T0383186

Out of the Box Thinking for Successful Managers

Out of the Box Thinking for Successful Managers

William F. Roth, PhD

CRC Press
Taylor & Francis Group
Boca Raton   London   New York

CRC Press is an imprint of the
Taylor & Francis Group, an **informa** business

A PRODUCTIVITY PRESS BOOK

CRC Press
Taylor & Francis Group
6000 Broken Sound Parkway NW, Suite 300
Boca Raton, FL 33487-2742

Printed on acid-free paper
Version Date: 20140703

International Standard Book Number-13: 978-1-4822-4706-0 (Hardback)

Visit the Taylor & Francis Web site at
http://www.taylorandfrancis.com

and the CRC Press Web site at
http://www.crcpress.com

This book is dedicated to
Russell L. Ackoff,
who taught us to question—
with thanks and with hopes that he can
finally slow down a little
and smell the roses…
while we carry on.

Contents

Preface

During my years spent in the corporate world, first as an employee, then as a consultant, and during the close to 20 years I have taught management theory at both the undergraduate and graduate levels, I have tripped continually over management practices that don't make much sense.

For example, why do so many companies have evaluation and reward systems that force employees to compete against each other while, at the same time, these companies preach the gospel of cooperation and teamwork? Why is Management by Objective (MBO) still so popular? Why do companies continue to downsize when this practice has been proven antithetical to long-term success? Why do we continue to pay homage to the Baldrige Quality Award criteria when so many companies that have shaped their cultures around these criteria, even companies that have won the award, continue to run into serious problems afterward? Why do executives keep flocking to the next version of Frederick Taylor's scientific management as the holy grail in terms of increasing productivity when all the versions previously introduced have fallen short, and for the same reason? Why do efforts to improve the ethical climate in organizations continue to focus on "converting" the individual employee, rather than on redesigning the processes that encourage, that sometimes even force, unethical behavior?

Some of these practices I have written about in books— *Quality Improvement: A Systems Perspective* in 1998; *The Roots and Future of Management Theory: A Systems Perspective* in 1999; *Ethics in the Workplace: A Systems Perspective* in 2005; *Comprehensive Healthcare for the U.S.: An Idealized Model* in 2010. A number of them I have addressed in articles, more than 50 at this point, which have appeared in a wide range of both national and international journals.

I don't know, however, if my books and articles, or if the books and articles and films of other professionals who are serious about encouraging change—the Peter Druckers, the W. Edwards Demings, the Russell Ackoffs, the C. West Churchmans, the Tom Peters, the Fritjof Capras, the Peter Checklands, the Gerald Midgleys, the Peter Senges—have had any real effect. Change is occurring, yes, but very slowly, too slowly.

A handful of companies have figured things out, have gotten rid of such practices as obviously counterproductive in terms of the long-term bottom line. Most of these companies are doing well. A much larger number of organizations, however, due at least partially to these practices and to the anxiety-producing work environment they create, have eventually imploded and gone out of business, which is not a good thing in terms of our overall economic health.

Eventually, I decided to combine a number of my articles into a book that addresses what I consider to be the major "sacred cows," or myths—the ones that managers need to seriously examine and eventually do away with or, at least, replace with a modified version that makes more sense.

Humans are creatures of habit. We grow accustomed to doing things in a certain way. Even when that way is proven to be outdated, even when we know that it is not producing the results that it used to, even when we realize that it has been wrong all along, that it has consistently generated negative consequences in terms of our long-term goals, we are reticent to change, suffering from the old "don't rock the boat" syndrome.

In *Out of the Box Thinking for Successful Managers* I try to show in a user-friendly manner why these myths are myths, why they are based on complete falsehoods in some cases and on worn-out logic that needs to be replaced in others. But the book doesn't stop there. After showing where the holes lie in these myths, the book offers alternative approaches, ones that encourage a more positive and productive workplace culture. For example, why don't we just get rid of the traditional performance evaluation all together? What role does it really serve other than to load one more responsibility onto already overburdened managers?

If that question doesn't pique your interest, I don't know what will.

Anyway, I hope that you enjoy the book and gain something of value from it.

Chapter 1

Six Sigma: Or, Here We Go Again

Six Sigma is all the rage now. MBA programs are teaching it; corporate executives are lining up to sing its praises; consultants, of course, are cashing in on it. But the flaws are beginning to show. Yes, it does indeed benefit organizations, at least initially. But then problems begin to arise, and employees start to wonder, "Could it be possible that Six Sigma is not all it has been cracked up to be?" Could it be possible? *Could it, in fact, be probable that Six Sigma is nothing new, that it is simply the latest volley fired against nonquantitative approaches by those locked into the numbers during a war that has been going on, believe it or not, since the mid-1700s?*

The mid-1700s was when Adam Smith, the father of modern-day laissez faire economics (also called the free enterprise system), included in his offering the concept of *division of labor.* Smith showed the business community that by breaking a production process down into the simplest possible steps and assigning each step to a different worker, productivity would increase. His motives were good. He thought that the increased profits resulting from this approach would be distributed to help all of society. At the same time, he wanted to make the unskilled employable. Those incapable of crafting an entire shoe could at least be trained to make one part of it. But Smith also commented that such an approach turned the people doing the work into "human beings as stupid and ignorant as it is possible for a human being to become." As we know, nothing comes for free.

Birth of the Mechanist and Human Relations Schools of Thought: The Battle Begins

And so, the battle was on. Those focused on the numbers, on efficiencies, evolved into the *Mechanist* school of thought that tried to quantify everything, then to manipulate the numbers in order to improve the bottom line. Members of this school believed that employees should be programmed to function as parts of a "well-oiled machine" with no need to think, fueled only by their pay. The other side of the battle was taken up by the *Human Relations* school of thought. Its members taught that rather than efficiencies, the focus should be on the employees, on identifying and meeting employee needs, on developing and effectively utilizing employee potential. The employees, in turn, would take care of the efficiencies.

Following Adam Smith, the next major contributor to the Mechanist approach was Frederick Taylor, who developed *Scientific Management* during the last part of the 1800s. To the workplace he introduced scientific method (observe, measure, repeat) as a vehicle for discovering the best way to break processes down into individual tasks, then for discovering the most efficient way to complete each task in terms of both the time and the energy expended. But a new twist was added at this point. While Adam Smith introduced division of labor as a way to make unskilled laborers employable, as a way to give them the means to earn a living by simplifying production steps to the point where the unskilled or uneducated could handle them, Taylor's emphasis was instead on eliminating as many employees as possible, on squeezing more productivity out of fewer workers so that the cost of labor would drop and bottom-line numbers would improve.

This, of course, didn't go over too well with the workers.

Another problem with Taylor's scientific management approach was that those standing at the machines, those behind the counter, or sitting at the desk did not appreciate being treated as machine parts and balked at doing what they had been trained to do. Frustrated by their attitude, Taylor was forced to seek ways to encourage employees to meet their required production numbers. He did so by adding an incentive system. After defining the most efficient way to complete each task and the time each repetition of the task should take, he calculated how much work could be completed in a day. If employees did things the right way and met their quotas, they would receive their normal salaries. If they exceeded these quotas, they would receive part of the extra profit generated as a bonus. This approach worked until top management started raising the bar in terms of quotas, claiming that the workers had been holding out and didn't deserve a bonus.

Advocates of the Human Relations school, during this time, were not sitting idly by watching. People like Robert Owen, then Elton Mayo, Chris Roethlisberger, Mary Follett, and Oliver Sheldon were preaching and demonstrating with positive bottom-line results that treating workers like human beings rather than brainless machine parts, meeting their needs, and encouraging development of their potential did indeed generate increased profits, though most members of the business community refused to listen.

Deming and the Systems Approach: Why, Indeed, Is Nobody Listening?

The next key figure in the evolution of the Mechanist school was W. Edwards Deming, who made his contribution during the middle and late 1900s. Deming built on Taylor's work, introducing statistics and a range of process definition and measurement techniques to better identify and deal with production process strengths and weaknesses. He also introduced the "plan-do-check-act cycle," a simple way to organize improvement efforts.

The way these tools and techniques should be used and by whom, however, according to Deming, again added something new. In Smith's model the workers were simply trained how to do their jobs; in Taylor's model quantitative tools were used to discover the most efficient way to complete a task and then the employees were taught that way; however, in Deming's model the employees themselves were trained to use the tools and techniques in order to find ways to improve productivity and to make their work more efficient.

Deming was also one of the first to straddle the boundary that separated his school from the Human Relations school, claiming that while his statistical measurement tools were valuable, they were just that, tools, and that the key was not so much teaching these tools as developing commitment in employees to use them effectively. In fact, he claimed that in terms of increasing productivity, these tools were only 10 percent of the package. The rest had to do with finding ways to generate commitment and to release the potential of workers.

Deming along with Peter Drucker, Russell Ackoff, Eric Trist, Fred Emery, C. West Churchman, Chris Argyris, Donald Schon, and a growing number of others were forming to a new school of thought, the *Systems school* that defined as one of its challenges mapping out ways to combine the strengths of the Mechanist and Human Relations approaches. The Systems school is also based on the concept that "a whole is more than the sum of its parts," which means that to understand how an organization operates, to understand how to improve that operation, we cannot go at it piecemeal; we cannot assign individuals or teams the task of improving the financial department, the information systems, human resources policies, the evaluation process. We must, rather, come up with a way to address all of these pieces of the puzzle at once in an integrated manner because the interactions between them are just as important or even more important to bottom-line improvement than the parts themselves.

One of the most important of these parts found in any organization is the employees and their needs, many of which are nonquantifiable. When we leave employees and their needs out, according to Systems theory, we are obviously neglecting a critical part of the puzzle.

But again, relatively few business leaders listened; or they listened but then dissected the strategies presented by the Systems school, ignoring the nonquantitative parts, focusing on the quantitative parts when striving to increase productivity. They did this because, quite simply, the nonquantitative parts did not make sense to them. For example, most people are familiar with Deming's statistical measurement techniques—histograms, cause-and-effect diagrams, flowcharts, run charts, control charts, scatter diagrams, Pareto diagrams. But how many have given more than a cursory glance to his 14 Points for Management? One of these points is to drive out fear. "But what's that about?" we wondered. "How do you define and measure fear?" Then again, another point is to break down barriers between departments. "But how do you do that?" we asked. "And how do you quantify the benefits of doing so?"

Hammer and Reengineering, or, Once Again with Feeling

While a growing amount of at least lip service was being paid to the nonquantitative side of the equation—the concept of *employee empowerment*, for example, appearing with increasing frequency in the literature—the quantitative approach still ruled. Its next manifestation was *Reengineering*, introduced in 1990 by Michael Hammer, a retired Massachusetts Institute of Technology professor who had taught computer science. Dr. Hammer's focus was on eliminating non-value-adding work. If an activity did not add value for the customer, get rid of it. Previously, he claimed, technology had been used to make all work more efficient without first asking whether or not that work was actually contributing to improvement of the bottom line. This, according to Dr. Hammer, should be the first question addressed.

Reengineering focuses on two things: making major improvements in existing processes, and promoting business innovation. Its most important tool for addressing both challenges is the information system. Reengineering starts at the top of the organization with an assessment of mission, strategic goals, and customer needs; then works downward, focusing on entire business processes rather than on parts of them, realizing, as the Systems school teaches, that to fragment these processes into their parts in order to address the parts individually would be to lose the vital interactions. But at the same time, by focusing on the key processes rather than on the organization as a whole, Reengineering still loses the interactions between the *processes*, so that the defined weakness remains, just on a different level.

Another thing borrowed by Reengineering from the Systems approach is its "clean slate" perspective. Instead of starting by identifying the weaknesses and strengths of the current process configuration, then prioritizing them and working to correct or enhance them, Reengineering wipes everything away and redesigns the process from scratch. This approach in the Systems world has been labeled "idealized design" and was developed initially by Russell Ackoff and C. West Churchman. The critical difference between these two versions is that while Hammer's clean slate approach involves mainly experts and upper-level managers, idealized design makes employees at every level responsible for redesigning their part of the operation and for making sure that the different designs complement each other, the exercise thus gaining the benefit of their expertise and experience as well as their commitment. Instead of getting rid of employees as a means of improving the bottom line through increased efficiencies as Reengineering does, the Systems approach improves the bottom line by taking better advantage of employee expertise and potential.

Creating an incentive system to generate employee commitment was not a major part of Reengineering, as it was with Taylor and is with the Systems approach. The focus was completely on increasing efficiencies, no matter what the cost to the numbers that represented employees. Enthusiasm for this approach lasted about five years, then faded rapidly as critics began to pick it apart.

Six Sigma, the Latest Kid on the Block

The next version of the Mechanist approach to hit center stage was the still popular Six Sigma. This approach borrowed a whole lot from many different sources. In many ways, it seems an updated repeat of Taylor's scientific management. Six Sigma was introduced by Motorola during the 1980s, again as a means of making manufacturing processes as consistent as possible and of reducing the rate of defects in finished products. But as the approach evolved, attempts were made to deal with management challenges as well.

Building on Deming's plan-do-check-act cycle, "project management approaches" were spawned by advocates. The two most popular were modeled on those offered by Reengineering. DMAIC, or "define opportunities, measure current performance, analyze weaknesses, improve performance, control the improved performance to sustain gains," was used to improve existing processes. DMADV, or "define opportunities, measure customer requirements and see what competition is doing, analyze options, design process, verify process performance" was used to create a new process. Both of these approaches were, again (like Deming's plan-do-check-act cycle), common sense and practice made explicit.

Six Sigma is data driven. In order to gather this data and use it to make improvements, an entirely new hierarchy is introduced to an organization. Modeled on the popular martial arts reward system, three of the five levels are designated by belt colors. At the top is the Quality Leader who is ultimately responsible for integrating the effort and for its success. Below are the Master Black Belts, responsible for a specific part or function of the organization—human resources, marketing, research and development, production, etc. Below that are the Process Owners, responsible for a specific process within a function, say, for training process in the human resources function. Next are the Black Belts, who lead improvement projects.

Everybody down to this level is totally dedicated to the Six Sigma effort in terms of time allocation; these people have no other responsibilities. Only the Green Belts, the lowest level, add their Six Sigma chores to their normal workload. The belief is that as workers become more familiar with the tools and techniques introduced, they will integrate them into their normal efforts so that less extra time is required.

Six Sigma is also similar to Taylor's model in that a reward system tied to productivity has been put into place. Starting at the bottom this time, Green Belts can be awarded gift certificates, bonuses, and stock options, depending on the benefit to the company of their work on projects. Black Belts and Master

Black Belts have their salaries and bonuses tied to the value of successful projects they have led. The compensation of process owners depends on meeting their process goals, as does that of the Quality Leader.

Training is important to this approach. Everybody receives several weeks of it. At the lowest level, the Green Belt level, students are introduced to more than 50 different tools and techniques including development of a process control plan, documenting a process, failure modes and effects analysis, value-added analysis, affinity diagrams, verification of root causes, measurement system analysis, understanding variation, gathering voice of the customer, and the Six Sigma language. Black Belts are introduced to more than 75 tools and techniques.

Not Much Has Really Changed

A lot of thought and a lot of study obviously went into the development of Six Sigma. It has borrowed from many of the best improvement models, starting with Frederick Taylor's scientific management. Six Sigma goes right up to the boundary separating the Mechanistic and Human Relations approaches. It includes employees from all levels in improving key processes; it works to integrate efforts; and it provides a reward system tied to bottom-line improvements.

But Six Sigma does not allow companies to cross over the boundary. Six Sigma is still top down, driven by management. Employees on all lower levels are told what to work on and how to address the challenges confronted; they are trained to use specific tools and techniques. Six Sigma does not make the most effective use of employees' expertise; it does not truly "empower" employees.

So, concerning the Mechanist school, not much has really changed. On the philosophical side the objective remains, quite simply, to improve efficiencies with the understanding that, by definition, such improvement can be measured only numerically. The changes in this school have occurred almost without exception on the practice side. They include increasing the number of tools and techniques brought into play, increasing the level of sophistication designed into these tools and techniques, and making the incentive system more sexy without taking into account the cultural change required by real empowerment.

The results of the Mechanist school's different approaches—scientific management, implementation of Deming's quantitative tools, Reengineering, Six Sigma—have also been basically the same. Companies have started out with impressive bottom-line improvements. But these results have tapered off due to the additional work involved, due sometimes to the lack of an appropriate reward system, and due sometimes to the effects of resultant layoffs on workforce morale. Enthusiasm has eventually died down, until the pieces have been once again rearranged or elaborated on, until the next approach has been put together with much fanfare and the cycle has gained new life, starting all over.

The Alternative and Why We Refuse to Take It Seriously

What is the alternative? How do the Human Relations- and Systems-based approaches go about improving the bottom line? Why are companies that use them highly successful, not just in the short term but in the long term? The best film I have ever seen on effective management was Tom Peters' 1994 *The Leadership Alliance*. It showed three companies—a Bay City, Michigan, General Motors components plant; Johnsonville Sausage; and Harley Davidson—that introduced the Human Relations/Systems approach, though they didn't call it that. In fact, these three companies didn't call it anything; they just turned the operation over to their employees and asked that the employees help improve their part of it, period.

No money was spent on consultants brought in to introduce a model and to train. In fact, no up-front training occurred. No special tools and techniques were introduced—the workers were designing or picking their own tools and techniques. Employees were simply given the authority to come up with improvements in their own areas of expertise and then to implement them, making sure that they first asked for input from other parts of the operation that might be affected. Management's role was not to direct the efforts of employee teams, but rather to facilitate and help integrate these efforts.

And that's it. Basically, that's all they did.

Other well-known companies that have enjoyed ongoing success using versions of this model include W. L. Gore, Semco in Brazil, L. L. Bean, Toyota, Whole Foods, Google, Whirlpool, and Wegman's Grocery. But the Human Relations/Systems model is not spreading very rapidly, most corporations still refusing to modify their Mechanist mentality. This brings us to our next questions: "Why," we must ask, "why aren't more companies eager to erase the boundary? Why aren't more companies willing to incorporate a healthy dose of the nonquantifiable into their efforts?"

The answer has at least four parts. The first part is that numbers are obviously a whole lot easier and faster to work with than people. They have no emotions; they do not grow confused, angry, or hurt. Executives can make very large, sweeping changes based on numbers without worrying about the details, though these details frequently turn out to be the determining factor.

A second part of the answer is that our education system, especially at the MBA level, continues to focus on the numbers, perhaps because professors can bring them into the classroom, building elaborate models on the blackboard that make perfect sense in this setting, that again, exclude all the nonquantifiable variables one must deal with in the workplace. It is a pretty safe bet, for example, that Reengineering was developed on a blackboard. Professors cannot, however, bring a workforce, the source of these missing variables, into the classroom—only case studies that can give students an intellectual sense of what went on, but not a real feel for it, the kind of feel that comes from being an actual participant.

A third part of the answer is that our economy is driven by the financial community, which is totally about numbers, about this quarter's improvement in the bottom line. Top-level managements are forced to focus on satisfying Wall Street's demands, on meeting the numbers. It is hard for them to think about anything else, their perspective definitely being skewed toward the quantitative.

A fourth part of the answer is our current evaluation and reward system that forces competition for advancement in most companies, especially at the managerial level. Managers are reticent to give control to their workers in case something goes wrong that can be held against them; they are afraid that if the workers do well they might become expendable; they are afraid to get away from the numbers that are the easiest proof of their productivity.

In conclusion, with these things in mind, it should be pretty obvious by this time that our approach to improving productivity in the business world is going to remain the same until we change some things. But, it should also be obvious that the changes we are talking about are going to require a fundamental shift in cultural emphasis, away from judging the value of everything quantitatively and toward a more balanced perspective. Finally, it should be obvious that such a shift, despite the hard lessons we have learned and are continuing to learn, seems to be very slow in coming.

Chapter 2

Downsizing: The Cure That Can Kill

Recently, a news report caught my attention. It concerned a company in Japan that, in order to save money during the worldwide recession, has everybody leaving the office and working outside for several hours each day so that the heat can be turned down. I smiled and thought, as I am sure quite a few people thought, Those crazy Japanese. But then I thought, Why would a company do something so bizarre? Wouldn't such a move interrupt work and cut down on efficiency? Wouldn't the employees rebel?

Eventually the realization dawned on me that top management in this organization, instead of being silly, were trying to find an alternative to laying employees off, layoffs being considered extremely disrespectful in the Japanese business culture, a strategy to be avoided whenever possible.

Another method used in that country to save jobs is to cut salaries so that nobody has to leave and everybody is still earning enough to survive. The first salaries to be cut are those of corporation executives, who publicly take responsibility for the downturn, apologizing to the workforce. This display of humility usually makes sense because executives are, in most cases, primarily responsible for a company's fortunes. At the same time, in that they are the most highly paid members of the staff, the salary reduction will hurt them less. Such an approach seems especially virtuous—and novel—in light of the recent reports of scandalous executive compensation payouts and perks in financially troubled US companies that have received taxpayer bailouts.

The Many Dark Sides of Downsizing

Because many US executives take the short-term view, looking for quick, "clean," uncomplicated savings to produce rapid improvements in the bottom line that will keep Wall Street happy, because they turn to Reengineering, Six Sigma, and other techniques focused totally on increased efficiencies, and because the quickest way to increase these efficiencies is to get rid of employees, the most popular response in this country to an economic downturn remains layoffs.

In order to take the burden of being the "bad guy" off top management, the directive for a layoff usually requires that a certain percentage of staff be cut from each department in order to "spread the pain," with lower-level managers being given the difficult and stressful task of deciding who must go.

But downsizing comes with hidden costs that don't show up until a little further down the road, these costs rarely figuring into a company's "what should we do in order to improve the short-term bottom-line" mathematics.

I teach in an MBA program. A while ago I asked a class of 23 students, all of whom currently held mid-level management positions and most of whom had lived through a downsizing at some point in their careers, what the effect of that downsizing was on their organization.

Access to information. The first thing they ran into, my students told me, was increased difficulty in getting the information needed to conduct the organization's business. They said that the remaining employees began to hoard information, the presumption being that if they were the only employee possessing it, they would be more valuable to the company and therefore harder to lay off. When others asked for such hoarded information, employees pretended not to have access to it. At the same time, because responsibility for files had been shifted, or because management, afraid that employees might misuse information, had labeled it confidential, files necessary to do one's job were more difficult to find or to gain access to. Those given responsibility for additional files were not familiar with them, and were frequently too busy to learn what was necessary in order to manage them properly.

The students also said that information coming down from top levels became suspect, as were requests from superiors for information. That flowing in from other parts of the organization was considered questionable as well, the suspicion being that it had been doctored to create a more favorable impression. A "law of the jungle" climate evolved, the students said, with people doing whatever they thought necessary to survive. Information was power; it was one of the few weapons they had at their disposal. Therefore, they used it in any way they saw fit.

Communication. The next thing the students observed was that in terms of communications, mistrust ran rampant. People read more than usual into everything they were told. The rumor mill took over as staff spent more time than usual gossiping about the suspicions flowing constantly through the organization. Most of the conjecture, of course, was negative—when the next round of layoffs might come (despite top management's assurances to the contrary), who would be next to go, etc.

Training. The students all agreed that following the downsizing everybody was overloaded with additional work, some or all of which they had not been trained to do. Their companies had tried to keep the decision to downsize quiet until the last possible minute and then, after the announcement was made, to get the laid-off employees out the door as quickly as possible. As a result, the survivors, who had to take on the responsibilities of those released, did not receive the training necessary to handle their additional tasks properly. The people best qualified to train them were now gone, so they were forced to do most of their learning on the job, through trial and error, under the burden of a heavier workload, afraid to ask for help, afraid to give the appearance of incompetence.

Problem solving and decision making. The students reported that risk minimization and avoidance took on new emphasis in their downsized organizations. Because nobody wanted to chance making a mistake, innovative thinking, when most needed, was set aside, and the focus shifted to pleasing the boss. With less access to needed information, with the breakdown in communication and organization integration, input important for problem solving and decision making was more frequently unavailable.

Rewards. Another casualty of downsizing that my students observed was the reward system. The remaining workforce, despite the added responsibilities taken on, received no raise in pay. Some employees, in fact, had to accept salary cuts. Management, when questioned, told them that their reward was continued employment—they should be happy to still have jobs. The employees, of course, did not look at it this way and resented the company's condescending attitude. Also, job security, possibly the most important reward in employees' minds, could no longer be considered a given, no matter what management said to the contrary. Individuals began sending out feelers, frequently on company time using company computers and telephones to see what other jobs were available— just in case.

Morale and engagement. Obviously, morale and engagement in these organizations was adversely affected by the downsizing and by the resultant breakdowns in key systems. From the employee's perspective, "Why should I work harder to complete my additional duties when I can't gain access to the information required, when I am not being paid more, and when I might be out of here in a couple of weeks anyway? Management has no respect for me. Why should I work myself to death trying to deliver what it is asking for?" According to my students, employees started missing work, taking sick days, vacation days, and then unpaid days off. Employees spent more and more time looking for other jobs and took the ones they could find, escalating the rate of turnover.

And so it goes, the dark side of downsizing spreading through the organization to adversely affect every system, every employee. Despite all the pep talks and promises made by upper-level management, the most common result of this tangle of key system breakdowns in most downsized organizations—disappearance of information, paranoia, stifled communication, the lack of training, the shrinking of rewards (both explicit and intrinsic)—turns out to be that productivity begins to fall and the bottom line, after an initial sharp upward spike, soon follows. The recovery time after downsizing has been estimated to be around two years. During that time, the additional profits gained from the layoffs are usually eaten up by inefficiencies. Companies frequently find themselves in trouble again, but with less of a chance to stabilize their bottom line by another round of downsizing.

Alternative Strategies for Cutting Costs

Other, more humane and less disruptive ways can reduce labor costs besides layoffs. The most reasonable of these is through attrition. When people retire or quit, the company does not replace them. Another way is to pay people to retire early. In this instance, the problem comes when more employees than expected accept the offer, leaving the company in a bind.

Companies can also call for a short, mandatory shutdown or encourage, sometimes even force, employees to use their vacation time or to take a furlough or a sabbatical. Some companies arrange for employees to work fewer hours or to work fewer days.

Salary reduction is another stopgap measure, one that requires employees to take a temporary financial hit, but one that can help a company stave off workforce reductions.

The purpose of these strategies is to reduce labor costs relative to revenue and to do so *without* incurring a devastating hit to productivity, without incurring the loss of expertise gained through expensive training and experience, without sacrificing synergies that have taken a long time to develop.

Let's take a look at a couple of companies that have put these strategies into action.

Nugget Market

Nugget Market, a highly respected, upscale grocery chain in California, is striving to avoid layoffs during the current recession by combining several staffing strategies that reduce workforce expenses the payroll can no longer support during business slowdowns. Kate Stille, director of marketing, told me that during downturns the company opts not to replace employees who leave. This does not, however, cause much of a problem because all staff in all the chain's stores have been cross-trained and are expected to jump in to help out wherever and whenever needed. Also, the stores in the chain share staff. If the workload is heavy at one store and light at another, people shift location. For busy seasons, such as the Christmas holidays, instead of hiring additional full-time workers, Nugget recruits temporary employees, such as college students home for break.

These are all relatively small adjustments to policy, but they give the company enough staffing flexibility to avoid having to take more drastic measures during business fluctuations.

Dorner Manufacturing Corporation

Dorner Manufacturing Corporation in Hartland, Wisconsin, a manufacturer of conveyors and related equipment, successfully avoided layoffs in the 2001 business downturn through a work reduction strategy. The current director of human resources, Ken Oeschsner, told me recently that as a result of a company-wide meeting about the impact of the current recession on Dorner, it was decided to once again implement this same job-saving strategy. Everybody, including top-level executives, has accepted a one-week layoff during each quarter until the economy turns around. Because all personnel in the company, from top to bottom, are taking the same hit, employees see this as fair. Workers are eligible for unemployment during that week.

As the recession deepened, the company found it had to take additional measures to further reduce its costs, and opted to implement a graduated pay reduction as well. To "equalize" the degree of sacrifice across the organization, the percentage of temporary salary reduction rose by 1 percentage point with each $10,000 increment in salary—beginning with no pay cut for those earning $50,000 or less, a 1 percent reduction for those making $50,000–$60,000, a 2 percent cut for the $60,000–$70,000 bracket, and so forth, maxing out at a 5 percent cut for those making more than $90,000.

Dorner discovered, however, that the combination of the quarterly temporary layoffs and people taking their normal vacation days was resulting in too much lost work time. Production was falling below demand. As a consequence, everybody was asked to give back a week of their vacation benefit.

Should Dorner eventually be forced to reduce its employee population, the sacrifices already made by the entire workforce will minimize the extent of the cuts.

The above alternatives, although preferable to downsizing, also have drawbacks. The attrition approach usually take a long time to produce the desired results, sometimes years.

Temporary layoffs, salary reductions, and benefit givebacks demand administrative dexterity. They entail some uncertainty about their effectiveness, about whether or not additional steps may be necessary. They also require dealing with difficult questions—Just how long is the pay cut going to last? How many more temporary shutdowns are we going to have? Should I begin looking for another job or try to hang on?—as well as closely monitoring the organization's emotional climate to ensure that employees keep their sacrifices in perspective.

It Seems That Downsizing Is the Result More of a Mind-Set than of Necessity

The technique of cutting labor costs through downsizing or other means is largely a focus on *efficiency,* a purely quantitative concept. A downsizing strategy sees employees as numbers to be manipulated, and erased if need be, to improve the bottom line. The alternative approaches described above, by the mere fact that they try to preserve jobs, demonstrate that the involved companies view employees as more than cost elements in the business. Nonetheless, these strategies still focus, as we have seen, on efficiency, on bringing costs in line with declining revenues.

In contrast to the narrow focus of efficiency, companies can construct workforce solutions in a downturn that focus on *effectiveness*, solutions that include not only efficiency but also nonquantifiable factors such as creativity, enthusiasm, dedication, and the desire for self-improvement. Effectiveness encompasses the ability of employees to use inherent or developed talents to help improve their organization's operations. From this perspective, employees, rather than being victims of the downturn, become allies in management's efforts to find strategies for dealing with shrinking demand, stagnant prices, higher energy costs, stiffer competition, or any other factor that threatens its performance and, frequently, the company's very existence.

Lincoln Electric

Lincoln Electric, considered the top US manufacturer of welding and cutting equipment, successfully redefined the roles of a number of employees beginning in the late 1980s and through the early 1990s to avoid layoffs during a downturn that worsened into the 1990–1991 recession. According to Roy Morrow, Lincoln Electric's current director of corporate relations, these employees were assigned to newly formed "Leopard Teams," which were trained and then sent out as part of the sales force to talk with potential customers. As part of their job during the sales calls, the Leopard Team salespeople looked for new applications for company products that would generate new revenue for Lincoln Electric.

Similar approaches have been used for years in Japan during economic downturns. A company will take employees out of jobs no longer bringing money into the coffers and assign them the task of coming up with ideas for improving products, sales strategies, the use of technology, management systems—anything they can think of that will boost organization performance. Rather than losing expertise and synergies through layoffs, Japanese companies find a different way to make use of employee talents to help the organization become more productive. Also important is the fact that these innovations can be carried forward, positioning the company to be an even stronger competitor when the economy rebounds.

International Paper's Louisiana Mill Goes All the Way

Several years ago, the International Paper Company (IPCo) "went all the way" in terms of putting together an alternative to downsizing. Corporate headquarters decided that it needed to cut costs. Orders were passed down from the CEO that every mill should improve profits by laying off workers. The Louisiana Pulp and Paper Mill, however, one of the corporation's 16 primary mills, decided to do things differently.

The mill manager, who had run the mill for 10 years, was one of the most respected managers in the company. In terms of performance, Louisiana was somewhere in the middle of the pack of IPCo plants. Up to that point, the manager's approach to management had been largely autocratic. But he was getting tired of the long hours and of making most of the decisions, a situation that would only worsen if he had to cut back the workforce. Instead, he ignored the CEO's directive and took a quite different tack, one quite innovative for the times.

With the help of internal consultants from the corporation's Department of Organization Planning and Development, the mill manager set up a network of 45 teams, representing every function in his operation. The teams met weekly for an hour with the following charge:

1. Develop a list of improvements that could be made in each area of expertise and in conjunction with adjoining areas.
2. Prioritize the list.
3. Design each improvement.
4. Take responsibility for implementing the design.
5. Monitor the results of each change and make necessary adjustments.

A set of ground rules, which will be discussed in Chapter 7, were established to guide and help integrate the efforts of the teams. Decisions were made by consensus. The teams did not have leaders but rather facilitators who guided the effort but were not allowed to involve themselves in the problem-solving effort itself.

Within three weeks of the initiative's launch, the first teams were up and running. Each team then generated a list of 30 to 40 projects, prioritized them, and began work on them.

As you might guess, this process precipitated a shift in the management culture at the Louisiana Mill. It is claimed by some that such a shift takes years. That is not true. If the process is introduced correctly, change can begin to occur after several months and will snowball rapidly, with impressive results. According to the mill manager, within a year the teams had competed on more than 250 projects, some of which saved or generated thousands and occasionally hundreds of thousands of dollars, and some of which helped develop new markets for the mill's paper products.

Whereas at the beginning of the process the mill sat somewhere in the middle of the pack of International Paper's primary mills in terms of profitability, merely two years later it was number one, twice as profitable as the second-highest-performing unit. Rather than downsizing, the mill manager was now hiring additional employees to handle the higher production volume needed to supply the new customers identified by improvement teams.

The Louisiana Mill developed an alternative to downsizing that produced positive long-term bottom-line results while avoiding the loss of expertise, that encouraged the improvement of key organization systems rather than their breakdown, that bolstered morale and engagement rather than destroying them. The Louisiana Mill's manager made a courageous decision to try something that was not the norm but that made a great deal of sense to him and to his workforce. He put into place a vehicle that continuously utilized all the employees' expertise to design and implement improvements in every part of the organization. As a result, the mill not only avoided downsizing and its fallout but also gained increased effectiveness of key systems, with the increase in turn translating into greater competitive strength and improved performance.

The lesson we can take from IPCo's Louisiana Mill, I believe, is that the best way to avoid downsizing is, quite simply, to utilize employee expertise *beforehand* in ways that will make it unnecessary. The mill manager was able to successfully buck the system and jump-start his organization after the order to downsize had been issued. However, if IPCo had found ways to take better advantage of employee expertise *before the fact* in order to increase both productivity and efficiencies, the company might have been able to *preclude* even the *threat* of downsizing. The key is to think proactively, not to wait until the crisis arrives to act.

Maybe as a Last Resort

Downsizing should be a last resort in the US corporate world, just as it is in most other developed nations. Unfortunately, despite the detrimental effect it has been proven to exert on key organizational systems, employee morale, and most importantly the long-term bottom line, downsizing remains the strategy of choice for most companies when faced with an economic downturn or when pressured by Wall Street to show short-term improved profitability.

Alternatives do exist. They might take a little more work and a little more time, but the benefits of that additional effort, of that additional time, rapidly become apparent, not simply in terms of money saved but also in terms of the long-term appreciation, commitment, and engagement of the workforce in response to management's demonstration of respect. The best of these alternatives, of course, is for companies to make such effective use of employee expertise and ingenuity in developing new products, finding new markets, improving processes, and instituting cost-saving measures that downsizing need rarely be a consideration—even in the harshest economic climate.

But how do organizations gain these desired employee contributions? What kind of workplace atmosphere should organizations create in order to do so?

One of the first things required, if organizations are serious in their desire to improve long-term productivity, is that they shift from a competitive to a cooperative environment, killing in the process perhaps one of the most sacred cows of all.

Chapter 3

The Myth That Competition in the Workplace Is the Best Way to Increase Productivity

If organizations eventually realize that downsizing isn't the answer to improvement of the long-term bottom line, if they eventually realize that downsizing inevitably comes back to bite them and to bleed them, if they realize that efficiency increasing tools and techniques provide only a partial solution, one that turns out to be short term, then what is the answer? How do we cut costs and/or generate the necessary increases in employee productivity? Should we break out the whips, the cattle prods? Should we introduce a bonus system? Or is the issue more deep seated than that?

I believe that the issue is more deep-seated, much more deep-seated, and that the most important change needs to occur in the organization's culture.

So, we start off with another loaded statement. Here's what I'm talking about. Especially in the world of business an ongoing controversy has raged for centuries as to whether it is more effective to encourage competition between employees in the workplace or cooperation among them. Though in modern times there is growing emphasis on team efforts, which, by definition, depend on cooperation, a great number of executives—Jack Welch, for example, recent CEO of General Electric and darling of the old boy crowd because he had the fortitude to base his decisions totally on the numbers—strive to create a competitive environment in the belief that competition brings out the best in employees, that it forces them to try harder, to think smarter.

This might be so, but I doubt it, suspecting that this attitude is largely a self-serving one that has to do more with oversized egos and a lack of emotional development than with improving the bottom line.

With this opinion presented as its preamble, the purpose of Chapter 3 is to show in a relatively simple manner why cooperation, in both the short and long run, is more effective than competition or conflict in terms of improving productivity.

Getting the Necessary Definitions in Place

First of all we need to define our terms—*cooperation, competition, conflict*. It has been said that we do what we are rewarded for doing. Cooperation occurs when people are rewarded for sharing information, for supporting and facilitating each other's efforts, for integrating expertise and activities in order to generate a result greater than the sum of individual contributions.

Competition and conflict are related. In order to have competition three things are required: The first is a set of "rules of the game" that all participants agree to. The second is a referee whose job it is to enforce the rules. If a rule is broken during the competition, the referee doles out a punishment to the offender. The third is a two-level reward system. On the first level we find a "win-lose" arrangement. Only one team can win the match. On the second level, however, we have a "win-win" situation. Everybody benefits from being involved. Professional athletes are paid for playing, win or lose. They also gain a great deal of respect due to their skills and status. While lower-level competitors in any arena, be it chess or soccer or hopscotch, do not usually receive pay, they benefit from the respect part. Also, they are developing their potential while competing.

Conflict can be defined as competition without rules, without a referee and with a one-level lose-lose reward system. Even though there might be a "winner," the person or group that wins, in fact, usually loses a great deal as well during the conflict, war being the ultimate example. Anything goes in a conflict situation. Because no rules are in place, participants do whatever it takes to prevail. And because there are no rules that participants can agree to, because even if there are rules that participants initially agree to follow, they cannot trust each other to abide by them once things heat up, trying to referee the match is usually a waste of time.

Finally, we have the really sad part. Because with conflict the goal is to win in any way possible, a lot of effort is put into destroying the other team's resources. For example, if a football game were run as a conflict rather than a competition, one of the first actions most likely would be to put the other team's quarterback out of action.

Now, a Really Simple Proof That Will Make Tough Guys' Blood Boil

During that part of our lives spent in the workplace we have only a limited amount of both *time* and *energy* to expend on our assigned duties. These resources can be spent either in a *positive* or a *negative* manner. Thinking positively, employees can spend their time and energy accomplishing work-related objectives and assisting co-workers in accomplishing their objectives. When people share their energy, when they combine it to achieve goals, as we have said, *synergy* occurs. This means that through the involved interaction, additional energy is generated, a bonus of sorts that also can be directed toward the task at hand. A great deal of synergy is found in workplaces where cooperation is encouraged and rewarded.

In organizations where the reward system encourages competition, however, there is obviously no synergy, so that bonus is lost. At the same time, much of our time and energy is consumed by negative activities. Employees are forced to spend time ferreting out "enemies," those who want to "beat" us in order to improve their own situation. Employees must keep close watch over these people and their activities, which take additional time and energy. If an enemy does mount an attack, say, badmouths you to a superior, defensive action must be taken. You must spend time with your superiors and everybody who will listen clarifying the situation. You will probably also want to counterattack to destroy or put the enemy on the defensive. For the best possible results, you must do both, which takes still more time and energy. The enemy, of course, is not sitting still. That person is also jockeying for position in the battle, negatively expending additional amounts of his or her limited time and energy.

On top of everything else, there is the preemptive strike strategy. In a competitive environment, when suspicions arise that somebody might be planning an attack, when one learns that a peer has access to possibly damaging information, when one realizes that a peer or report is making a better impression on supervisors, the strategy is to attack first to neutralize the threat.

An extreme example would be Harry's experience. Harry's first job after earning his MBA was as a member of the human relations staff of a Fortune 500 company. Harry was full of ideas. He wanted to make a real contribution and discussed his ideas freely with peers. Eventually, he was invited to lunch by the supervisor of an adjacent function that would be affected by the improvements he had in mind. This person was a young woman named Eileen, who was considered to be an extremely intelligent, hardworking, "rising star" in the company. Eileen was charming. She was also extremely interested in his ideas, asking question after question, then suggesting that he write his thoughts down so she could study them and help him identify ways to present them to upper-level management.

Several weeks later, as you might guess, Harry was fired. He eventually learned that Eileen had engineered his demise, that she had then presented the ideas as her own.

Harry obviously did not understand the environment he was entering. He was assuming that employees there would be rational. If he had understood, our hero would have told nobody about his ideas; he would have waited the number of months or years it took to rise to a level of power and under-standing where he could protect them, or where he could at least deal with threats like Eileen.

This was an experience awash in negative time and energy. It is also a given that in his next job Harry shared as little as possible and was constantly on guard, expending the time and energy necessary to inspect his defenses daily, striking immedi-ately when the smallest suspicion of an impending attack arose.

Sad but True

A very sad and rather depressing truth is at play here, one that we have not been able to deal with effectively in our culture due to the unflagging influence of the "tough guys": *When competition and cooperation clash in pursuit of the same goal or in pursuit of related goals requiring the same resources, competition usually wins.* Cooperation is based on giving, on sharing, on working together; but competition is based on taking as much as possible while giving as little as possible in return. What would have happened in our scenario if Eileen, instead of destroying Harry so she could take credit for his ideas, had put the energy used to do so toward enriching the ideas with her own, toward helping him organize them so they could be presented effectively? What would have happened if she had suggested that they talk to other employees, gained their input as well? I can only assume that the results would have been far more positive for the company and for everybody involved, including Eileen.

A necessary follow-up question is, *How much time and energy does one believe the typical employee misuses in this manner?* Our answer would have to be, *Does it matter?* Every minute spent on defensive maneuvering is wasted or counterproductive in terms of improving the bottom line; and the minutes add up quickly.

Where Does It Come From?

Where does this attitude come from, this negative attitude that can rapidly infect everybody in an organization? We know that most people aren't normally that way. Outside the workplace—at home, in the community—stress is usually on cooperation. Most people participate in team sports while growing up. The coaches teach that the winning team is the one with members who work together, the one that combines member talents in the most effective manner. Players compete for positions on the team, yes, but it is a positive type of competition, one from which every player as well as the team benefits. It is the type of activity that allows development of each player's full potential. Once the game starts, however, team members stop the internal competition and focus on cooperating.

The Japanese management system is built around this principle. Cooperation is a workplace given; to compete with other employees is considered disgraceful behavior. The competition is saved for interaction with other companies in the local marketplace, but especially for interaction with other countries in the world marketplace.

So what happens in the US workplace? Why is the emphasis so often on the individual beating all comers, on competing when we have been raised in an environment that stresses cooperation? What happens when we walk into our office building or manufacturing plant? What do we leave at the door so that the workplace frequently becomes a battleground with no real rules, no real referees?

And why are the people who encourage this sort of behavior, the Jack Welchs, the bankers and brokers on Wall Street who engineered our recent economic collapse, looked up to and praised by so many in executives circles, at least until they get caught? What makes those people what they are; what makes them admirable?

I suspect that at least part of the answer has to do with what has been labeled "hotdogism."

The Cult of the Coney Island Hot Dog

So, what am I talking about with this hotdogism? A good way to start my explanation might be by offering another real-world example. This time, I'll talk about Jake. Our hero is an up-and-coming, low-level executive who works for a well-known truck manufacturing firm. He was recently given the task of leading the quality improvement process. Jake immediately established himself as the link between the quality task force and upper-level management. He made it clear that all accomplishments and failures were to be reported to him. He would make sure that they reached the right ears.

Jake then took it upon himself to personally carry the accomplishments "upstairs." When it came to failures, he assumed individual responsibility for meting out blame and punishment. He was constantly making very visible decisions, reporting almost daily to his superiors.

Jake soaked up as much credit and recognition as he could from the process. Then, when it began to falter due to poor design and flagging employee commitment (lower-level employees receiving very little feedback concerning their efforts), he hurried off to his next assignment, leaving the mess for his successor to clean up.

Jake is what we call a corporate hot dog. Such hot dogs are found in every type of organization. They've been given a variety of names, but I'll refer to them here simply as hot dogs in honor of the immortal Coney Island hot dog that drips with mustard, relish, onions, and sauce but upon closer inspection contains very little meat.

Hot dogs are hard workers; they spend long hours on the job. They will do just about anything or sacrifice just about anything or anyone to advance their careers. They are involved in everything, forcing their way into the lead. They love to deliver reports, give speeches, and be in the spot-light. They are very adept at stringing all the right buzzwords together. Hot dogs never take chances or say anything that might raise their boss's eyebrows. They are the consummate yes-men and women.

Most of us can live with that (people have learned to live with torture as well). Of greater concern, however, is the hot dogs' treatment of peers, and especially of subordinates. For hot dogs, life is one fierce competition. They do what they must to win. Peers are perceived as the enemy. Those report-ing to the hot dog are viewed as part of the hot dog's ammu-nition, to be expended as seen fit.

Hot dogs never see lower-level employees as a responsibil-ity. For example, hot dogs are very good at downsizing. They are frequently the ones to suggest it as a solution—a safe sug-gestion because downsizing (as we have said), despite mount-ing evidence that it rarely produces the desired long-term results, is still an accepted practice in corporate circles. Hot dogs frequently volunteer to be the hatchet man or woman, the bearer of bad tidings, because this role enhances their feeling of power over others while proving to superiors that they are a company person, willing to take on the unpleasant assignments.

On a day-to-day level, the hot dog manager, while polished in appearance and manner, is extremely demanding and tends to manage by fear, pulling reports aside to talk earnestly about their suspicion that the employee is not a real "team player." Hot dogs are also very good at lowering the carrot and promising whatever is convenient at the moment, with no intention of following through.

A second major concern is hot dogs' success in the current workplace environment. They are excellent at ferreting out what upper-level management wants to hear and offering this instead of the hard truth. Truth telling is left to others; the hot dog remains neutral, taking as much credit as possible when things work out, and pointing a finger when they don't.

Hot dogs tend to make a lot of enemies on the way up. As a result, when they have forged ahead of the pack, they immediately begin to get rid of those seen as threats. All those considered suspicious are dismissed, replaced by workers who have proven their loyalty, as well as by other hot dogs who are easier to deal with because the boss knows their game. Subordinates displaying real expertise and good ideas are kept around to be milked. But the hot dog boss makes sure that he or she receives credit for their contributions.

Rationalizations Pile On

The hot dog scenario is not a nice one, and it doesn't make much sense. But in too many cases, as readers know, it is workplace reality. Hot dogs are not new; they have been around since at least the inception of the free enterprise system. The first great apologists for this breed were perhaps the early Italian humanists who, during the Renaissance (1400s), in their efforts to gain release from the economic constraints imposed by the Catholic Church and the feudal state, reverted to the humanistic philosophy of the ancient Greeks. This philosophy stated that people should be allowed and encouraged to realize and enjoy their positive human potential to the fullest possible extent.

Emphasis during the Renaissance was mainly on the realization of economic potential. With this in mind, the early Italian humanists added their own twist to the Greek assertions and came up with what is now called Machiavellian humanism. They decided that businessmen should not need to let anything or anyone stand in the way of the realization of their economic potential, that businessmen should not have to worry afterward about the effects of their activities on others.

Rationalizations for the behavior of self-centered hot dogs kept piling up. John Calvin's theory of predestination espoused during the Protestant Reformation that followed the Renaissance (1500s) became one. It stated that our fate after death was predetermined by God, so that what we did during our lifetime didn't really have much bearing. Hot dogs during the Reformation, therefore, were free to do their thing without fear of repercussions.

During the ensuing Enlightenment period (1700s), the previously mentioned Scottish economist Adam Smith's theory of laissez-faire economics, if interpreted in a certain way, provided yet another excuse for such antics. Its core concept was that *the greatest good would come to the greatest number if society allowed every individual to pursue his or her own selfish economic interests.* The laws of nature, specifically *the law of supply and demand,* would keep things in balance. Smith, of course, later gave voice to his fear that the "monopolists" (a sixteenth-century term for hot dogs) would try to pervert these laws to their own benefit, that the activities of these people needed to be regulated. But this part of his argument was ignored.

More rationalizations appeared during the early Industrial Revolution (1800s) when the *social Darwinists* applied Charles Darwin's theory of evolution to the economic sector, proclaiming that humans in the workplace should behave like any other species and bow to the law of the jungle, that the strong should be allowed to exploit the weak in any way seen fit, and that such behavior must be condoned if we were to keep our economy strong.

In more modern times, Nobel Prize–winning economist Milton Friedman could be considered a spokesman for the hot dog school of thought with his defense of the pure laissez-faire approach, though it no longer exists anywhere in the world, and though history has proven its limitations over and over again.

The point is that hotdogism has not only survived but has flourished over the centuries. Today hot dogs abound in our world of business, battling their way up the modern organizational ladder until they reach that level at which they are home free, at which their smoke screen becomes impenetrable, at which they largely control their own activities and can keep a sizable number of people jumping through hoops so that the mirage of tremendous productivity is maintained.

What Do the Psychologists Say Concerning the Roots of This Behavior?

Now we can return to the original question: What makes these people what they are? Where does it come from, this workplace minority that has such a devastating effect on morale and productivity, that differs so greatly from you and me? (I assume at this point that any hot dog who began reading *Out of the Box Thinking for Successful Managers* has long since chucked it into a trash can.)

By way of explanation, anybody in the workplace possesses three basic types of skills. The first are *professional skills*, be they in the areas of accounting, engineering, marketing, or research. The second type includes *systems skills*. These give employees the ability to effectively utilize organization systems—such as the management system, the training system, the communications system, the access to information system. The third set, *political skills*, includes the ability to manipulate others so that they will do what you want them to do. This is not always a bad thing. Good managers have to be good manipulators.

A reasonable balance between the three sets of skills is generally sought. Some people, however, those labeled "politicians" by their peers and "hot dogs" by us, spend most of their time trying to manipulate others to improve their own situation exclusively rather than their own situation as part of a larger whole. A psychological theory concerning their disposition is based on developmental stages. The phenomenon we are talking about has been labeled *adolescent arrest.*

In the animal world (which includes humans), adolescence is a period of testing, competition, and occasional conflict. Young animals moving toward adulthood test themselves against each other and against adults (especially their parents) to discover and hone their strengths; to discover and work on their weaknesses; and to see how they fit into the pack, the herd, the group, or the society.

In terms of Abraham Maslow's famous hierarchy of needs, discussed in his book, *Motivation and Personality* (1954, 1970), we are talking about the fourth-level need to gain esteem that "leads to feelings of self-confidence, self-worth, strength, capability, and adequacy; of being useful and necessary in the world." Maslow continues, saying that "the thwarting of these needs, however, produces feelings of inferiority, or weakness, and of helplessness. These feelings, in turn, give rise to either basic discouragement or else compensatory or neurotic behavior."

Those successful in working through level four during adolescence move on to Maslow's fifth level, the quest for self-actualization. Activities at level five are generally more peaceful and cooperative. Those who get stuck at level four, however, frequently become hot dogs and spend the rest of their lives trying to beat everyone else on the block, everybody they come into contact with, to enhance their insufficient self-esteem.

At the same time, because the majority of us mature and move on into a more cooperative stage, and because cooperation involves giving as well as taking, those who remain stuck in their quest for self-esteem, those who suffer from adolescent arrest, enjoy an advantage. They see other's willingness to give as a weakness to be taken advantage of—and attempt to do so, usually successfully. As we have said, when cooperation goes up against competition or especially conflict, cooperation tends to get squashed, which is a major part of the reason productivity-improving efforts fail. Employees are told they have to cooperate with each other. Those who take the challenge seriously get misused by the hot dogs (Eileen, Jake and company) and eventually become cynical, even scared. Hot dogs see such efforts the same way they see every other effort, mainly as a means of improving their own status and of grabbing a larger share of the spotlight. Therefore, instead of striving to become a productive member of the team, they immediately begin to corrupt the process with their machinations.

It's Going to Take Radical Therapy

Can we change the current scenario? Can we lessen the negative impact of the hot dog element? We can't change the hot dogs themselves—that's a job for a therapist. But we *can* change the way we design relevant organizations' systems so that hot dogs lose their ability to move up, so that they eventually realize the need to change their attitude, style, or perhaps vocation.

Actually, it's quite simple. Hot dogs progress by focusing solely on the needs and desires of bosses, pretty much ignoring those of reports. They also keep moving around in an organization or between organizations so that no one has time to build and present a solid case against them. Once hot dogs have clawed their way up to a certain level in the hierarchy, they are difficult to dislodge. The key, therefore, is to block their upward progress. The best and possibly only way to do so is to make that progress dependent on the will of those who best understand their motives. The people we are talking about are not their bosses. Rather, they are the employees who have worked with and for them.

One currently popular instrument that moves us in this direction is the 360-degree performance evaluation. Employees critique the performance of managers as well as peers in the same manner that managers and peers critique their performance.

A weakness of all evaluation systems up to this point in history has been the time they take, especially for managers who may be responsible for 10 or 15 or 25 or 50 employees. The 360-degree evaluation system takes even more time than the others, much more time when we add up all the hours spent by everybody involved.

The most serious problem with the 360-degree approach, however, is not the time expended but that it is open to political maneuvering. While a good manager will welcome the opportunity to discover ways to improve his or her performance, the hot dog will do whatever possible to ensure that employees say the right thing. Subtle threats, bribery, and playing one employee against another are common tactics. No matter what reports say, or want to say, they must remember that the boss still has the power.

New World Thinking

Now I am really going to get crazy. A second, more logical, more effective approach to blocking hot dogs is to allow the employees of a unit to decide who their leader should be (I can see the bristles going up on the backs of necks). But think about it: Reports and peers should be best qualified to identify hot dogs. The upper-level bosses have very little opportunity to discover what is really happening in the trenches. As we have said, hot dogs are very good at blocking bad news and shaping their boss's views. But lower-level workers know absolutely what is going on, and who is doing what to whom, because they are intimately involved on a minute-to-minute basis.

Shapers of modern-day management theory have puzzled over the fact that in a society that proudly proclaims the effectiveness of the democratic form of governance to all who will listen, most of our businesses are run as dictatorships at worse or by a small, powerful elite at best. One explanation for this phenomenon is that until fairly recently most businesses were begun by one person or one family. They were built primarily to increase the fortunes of that person or that family. As a result, owners took responsibility for all of the important decisions.

Later, when companies were sold to the public through stock offerings so that they could grow, those placed in charge, though no longer the owners, were frequently reluctant to give up the sense of control and the privileges ownership entailed.

Peter Drucker said that for the industrial society that emerged following World War II to survive, it must give its citizens social status (an acceptable identity), a social function (a meaningful role), and decision-making power (democracy). He believed that the corporation offers the best institutional model for providing these things, but that the weak spot was democracy, especially in terms of the workforce. Drucker threw out the challenge of developing a model that would make organizations more democratic. What do we mean by "more democratic?" According to the experts, a democracy is a system of governance where those being led exercise control over their leader. They choose that person and are given the power to also remove said person if his or her performance is not acceptable.

If we eventually succeed in making organizations more democratic, the hot dog problem will be resolved. But of course, to get rid of the hot dogs and to have democracy flourish in the workplace, we must first get rid of our competitive climate so that employees will be willing to vote for somebody other than themselves. And of course, the thing most responsible for generating competition in the workplace is our traditional approach to evaluation and reward. Updating our evaluation systems and our reward systems must be a priority if we really want the involved changes to occur.

Chapter 4

Is It Possibly Time for Management by Objective to Bite the Dust?

Of all organization systems, as we have said, evaluation and reward do the most to shape a workplace culture. A majority of the traditional evaluation models currently in place create competition between employees on all levels—competition for the raise, competition for the promotion—impeding efforts to encourage cooperation and to increase productivity.

The good news is that a growing number of companies are developing evaluation systems that *do* encourage cooperation. The bad news is that although the positive results of this transition are obvious, most organizations continue to cling to traditional models.

The most popular of these models has, for many years, been *Management by Objective* (MBO), developed by Dr. Peter Drucker as a means of integrating the work of employees on all levels and of making sure that this work supports organizational objectives. *Although MBO was at one time useful, due to a rapidly changing workplace environment and to changing workplace needs and values, it has lost much of its usefulness and too frequently generates counterproductive results.*

So, here we go again, with a loaded statement that will startle some and anger others, that requires an in-depth explanation if I am going to get people to accept it.

MBO as a Starting Point

Dr. Peter Drucker, one of the founding fathers of modern-day management theory, made a number of valuable contributions during his career. One was MBO, an approach to employee evaluation and motivation. MBO begins when employees sit down with their immediate supervisors and outline goals for the following period. These goals normally focus on two areas. The first is the employee's productivity in terms of his or her responsibilities. This includes the number of sales made, reports filed, errors committed, projects completed, and new skills acquired. The second area concerns the way the employee performs. It covers the ability to take responsibility, to make decisions, to communicate effectively with others, to function as a team member, and to deal with customers. One approach to this exercise is for both the employee and the manager to create a list of goals for the employee, then to compare and negotiate.

At the end of the period specified—perhaps six months or a year—the two sit down again and go over the goals set out, discussing the degree to which each has been met. If the employee has fallen short, the reasons are discussed. The supervisor takes all this into consideration while later writing the employee's evaluation, which in turn contributes to decisions concerning pay raises, promotions, and discipline. The employee is asked to sign the evaluation, but before doing so can negotiate questionable sections. The employee also has the right to submit a rebuttal if he or she continues to disagree, the rebuttal being considered along with the evaluation before decisions concerning the employee's future are made.

MBO was first introduced by Dr. Drucker in his 1954 book entitled *The Practice of Management.* The logic behind this technique, as we have said, stems from Drucker's desire to integrate employee efforts and to tie these efforts to the strategic, long-term objectives of the organization. A cascading effect is supposedly created, top-level executives defining their goals in terms of corporate strategic objectives, those on the next level defining theirs in terms of the top executives', and so on down the chain of command. In this manner, the organization's overall perspective is not lost, with the goals of each level supporting those of the level above and those of the organization as a whole.

Challenges of a Rapidly Changing Workplace

We must remember, however, that this was 1954, less than 10 years after World War II had ended. Corporations in the United States were growing rapidly. A top-down, strictly hierarchical structure with clearly defined up-and-down reporting lines as well as communication lines helped keep growth under control. So, MBO fit the culture, even when Dr. Drucker pushed it beyond traditional limits by insisting that employees participate in the defining of their goals, whereas previously, based on the work of Frederick Taylor, the father of *scientific management*, such goals had been set by management.

Since that time, radical changes have occurred in the workplace, in management theory, and in management practices. In those days, due to the fact that both European and Asian manufacturing sectors had been destroyed, leaving the United States as the only producer on the block, buyers were lined up. Emphasis was on speed and efficiency, on "getting it out the door" as quickly as possible. The hierarchical model supported this emphasis. But now that quality has become just as important as speed, maybe even more important, now when we are learning that improved quality derives primarily from employee commitment, cooperation, and creativity, the hierarchical model of organization design is falling into disfavor because it is too inflexible. Things take too long to get done. Also, it encourages territorialism, the building of "silos," a cultural characteristic antithetical to comprehensive organization improvement, one frequently antithetical to much-needed innovation.

The team approach is now coming into its own with a call for open access to information, participative decision making, employee empowerment, and a reward system based on team and organization productivity as well as that of individuals. The question we must ask, therefore, is, *Does MBO in its current form continue to contribute to the effectiveness of all three—the individual, the team, the organization as a whole? Or, Does MBO work as well in this new world as it did in the old?* My answer would have to be, *I don't think so.* In fact, in some ways I believe that MBO is a barrier to the new culture evolving.

Why MBO No Longer Belongs at the Table

First, due to the ever-increasing rate of change in markets, in technology, and in societal trends, due to the growing amount of turbulence found in the business world, this year's goals defined during the initial part of an employee's MBO exercise might be obsolete within months, weeks, or even days. Carrying on in spite of these changes, still trying to meet them, hoping that one's period-end explanation of reasons for failure will be accepted, does not make much sense. The other alternative is for the employee to return to the supervisor and try to renegotiate the signed agreement. But the supervisor has perhaps 10 or 20 or 50 reports, and with the increasing volatility of the corporate environment, both internal and external, it may be necessary for each report to repeat this process on several occasions during the evaluation period, consuming large amounts of both employee and supervisor time and energy.

At the same time, measuring individual productivity is becoming increasingly difficult as organizations grow more sophisticated, as responsibilities grow more interdependent. It was easy to understand who contributed what to putting an automobile together in an early Ford Motors plant. It is not so easy in today's modern, information-driven corporation to differentiate between the contributions of the individual employees to growth in sales, to a report on new technology, or to the design of a more effective accounting procedure. The only way for this to occur would be for the supervisor to stand over each employee daily, watching to see just how much that employee does, indeed, contribute. Enough said.

The core problem here is the focus of MBO on *individual* performance, on defining individual goals for the period. Those goals might include the ability to work effectively with others, but they are still individualized. The employee is being graded on how well he or she works with others, not on how well team members as a whole work together, not on how productive the team is. In fact, the achievement of such individualized goals, which supposedly helps determine the employee's future, forces competition. "I want to be seen as the most cooperative member of the team. Therefore, I must *compete* with my fellow team members to see who can be the most *cooperative.*" Or, "My objectives have somehow come into competition with yours. Sorry about that, but because my career depends on how well I meet my objectives, I am going to do whatever is necessary." Such individualization is ultimately a barrier to improvements in productivity as well as in quality, both of which must feed off a truly cooperative environment if real success is to be achieved.

Third, we have the issue of *creativity*, which is growing increasingly critical in terms of excelling in the world market. When employees sit down to define goals with their supervisor, they tend to be conservative, to play it safe, not wanting to commit to anything they might not be able to accomplish. At the same time, spelling out what is to be accomplished puts boundaries around progress, sets up directional signposts, and focuses perspective so that if a new opportunity *does* materialize, something that might be risky but might benefit both the employee and the company, more than likely it will be ignored, first by the employee and also by the supervisor with whom it is shared. I have actually heard a mid-level manager, when approached by a report with a suggested improvement, say, "You know your responsibilities; we outlined them together. I suggest you pay attention to them, that you focus on meeting them." The manager was not being unkind or dictatorial; he was just trapped in the "well-oiled machine" mentality, afraid that if he allowed this one report to do something she was not "programmed" to do, others might want to follow suit and then his control as a manager would evaporate— control being the key to success in the hierarchical model.

Finally, when employees' goals have been predetermined and employees are driving forward, they will frequently work around problems encountered that do not directly hamper their progress toward MBO objectives, considering these problems as obstacles to be avoided rather than challenges to be met for the good of the company. Emphasis is on *me* meeting *my* goals rather than on *me* remaining flexible and doing whatever it takes to make the company as a whole more successful.

Once Again, What Is the Alternative?

Where does this leave us? Most modern-day evaluation systems include MBO, or at least the core characteristics of MBO. Most, therefore, hamper our efforts to continuously improve productivity and the quality of products, manufacturing or service processes, management systems, and the work environment. But without some tool of this sort, how do we evaluate employee effectiveness; how do we encourage employees to improve their performance?

One suspects that a direct correlation might exist between well-integrated employee contributions, improved productivity, improved quality, and improvement in the bottom line. Generally, the leaders in terms of profitability are those companies where employees have access to any information needed to support their efforts; where they are encouraged to make the decisions in their areas of expertise; where they have a voice in all decisions that will affect them, including who gets the promotion; where they have the authority to set and redefine their goals on a daily basis, to attack problems that crop up immediately with the organization's support; where the individual employee's reward is truly tied to the success of the company as a whole; where the evaluation and reward systems are designed to make them eager to cooperate, to share expertise; where teams are given the authority to hire new members and to counsel, discipline, and even to fire those whose performance is found lacking. We have all, by now, read about at least some of these leading companies. Fortunately, the list continues to grow.

Evaluation techniques, however, including MBO, have traditionally failed to encourage many of these things. Their role has been much simpler. It has been to enhance performance, to improve the employee–manager relationship, to provide a rationale for the distribution of raises, to decide promotions, and to document the need for discipline. But in organizations where management systems do possess the above-defined characteristics, improved performance is constantly being encouraged not only by supervisors but by everybody; managers are now *part* of the team rather than out in front giving directions and deciding who is good at what. Raises are tied to the success of the company rather than to the supervisor's largely subjective opinion; promotions go to the people who will benefit the team the most; discipline is now a responsibility of team members and is an ongoing, daily process.

W. L. Gore

One of the companies that does not use MBO is the well-respected W. L. Gore and Associates, which has been cited as a model for many things—creativity being one, project-based production being another. Though this company still has an employee evaluation system, their system incorporates many of the characteristics discussed above. Also, it is not built around MBO.

At W. L. Gore the process begins at the bottom rather than at the top. Instead of the boss sitting with the employee to define objectives and acting as the final judge concerning the employee's value to the company, team members evaluate each other, ranking peers on their contribution to the project assigned. Team members are also asked to explain the rationale behind their ranking and to comment on the strengths of each peer as well as areas where improvement can be made.

This approach combines cooperation with competition. While team members might compete to see who makes the most valuable contribution, they understand that their future ultimately depends on what is produced and that the best outcome will be achieved if they cooperate and combine their expertise.

This approach obviously encourages contribution to the team. It does not in any way limit reaction to unexpected opportunities. It encourages creativity. It does not tempt employees to sidestep problems. It gives team members incentive to adapt rapidly to changes in their internal and external environments. But at the same time, management still has the final say regarding who gets the largest raise, who gets the promotion, who stays employed. Management is still the final judge at W. L. Gore, and so the level of empowerment we have been talking about is not fully realized.

Bidding Farewell to a Player Whose Time Has Passed

MBO, unfortunately, as most traditional evaluation systems, feeds competition between employees. It is therefore turning into an obstacle as US companies move away from the top-down, boss-driven, hierarchical management model and toward one of the more flexible, team-driven alternatives necessary to success in the modern-day world of business. Chances of modifying it enough to make it work are limited; nothing would be left.

The only alternative, then, is to find another way.

Chapter 5

Get Rid of Performance Appraisals

Change is in the air; everybody is talking about it, trying to deal effectively with it, and for good reason. Donald Schon, in his 1979 book *Beyond the Stable State*, explained that the rate of change in our environment is increasing constantly. Dealing with it is becoming our major challenge. To do so in the realm of business we must develop organizations that are capable of learning continually from their environment and adapting. But how is that possible?

The best approach, of course, is to get everybody on all levels—workers and managers—involved. After the information is brought in, how do we make sure it reaches the right eyes and ears? And then, once it reaches the right eyes and ears, how do we ensure that it is used effectively?

In order to survive and then to thrive, our management systems need to be participative (in the real sense), well integrated, and finally, designed to encourage continual learning on all levels so that employees are skilled information gatherers, skilled disseminators, and skillful users. Employee commitment is critical to the success of such a culture, and one of the major obstructions to the generation of such commitment as well as to the necessary integration of efforts is the way employees are evaluated and rewarded.

Quite simply, organizations that are seriously interested in long-term bottom-line success should *consider getting rid of their traditional performance appraisal system* because it usually does more harm than good.

Again, this is a loaded statement, but I am not the only one who believes this. The same sentiment has been voiced by W. Edwards Deming and a number of other guides in our slow, painful transition to a new management style based on facilitation and teamwork rather than on in-house competition and rigid hierarchies—our transition to the new management philosophy made necessary by today's increasingly competitive economic environment.

Largely a Waste of Time?

The performance evaluation was created to facilitate the free-enterprise system. Advocates believed that those who work the hardest and most effectively, those who contribute the most, should benefit the most both financially and in terms of advancement. The evaluation system was created to define the individual's contribution level so that the reward level could be made to match it.

As the workplace culture progressed, other uses were added until, today, such evaluations serve five purposes as previously mentioned:

1. They are supposedly the major factor in determining the additional amount received when raises are given.
2. They are used to help determine who gets promoted.
3. They are used to help improve employee performance.
4. They allow the employee and manager to spend time together on a one-to-one basis, hopefully improving the involved relationship.

5. They provide documentation when disciplinary action is required.

Unfortunately, modern-day workplace reality negates most of these purposes. As we all know, the compensation awarded to top-level managers rarely has anything to do with their productivity. Rather, it has to do more with an ability to manipulate the numbers, the focus being on short-term profit no matter what the cost in the long term. Those making the decisions are locked into this focus, not so much because they are inherently shortsighted and greedy (although there is plenty of that) but because of the never-ending pressure from Wall Street.

At the same time, when we get real about it, being able to define a level of productivity down in the trenches no longer matters that much either. Rather than being based on individual productivity, raises are increasingly based on the amount of budgetary moneys allocated; this money is split as equally as possible first among the departments to avoid friction, and then the departments split it as evenly as possible among the employees to avoid hard feelings.

This means that Harry, who carries his normal workload but does little else, might receive a 2.5 percent raise, Mary, who has busted her buns and spent a lot of time taking on additional work, might receive a 3 percent raise—the difference in the dollar amount gained being almost irrelevant.

The manager's major concern in most cases, as has been said, is how to allocate salary increases in a way that will upset the smallest number of people rather than how to define which employees have contributed the most so that they can be rewarded accordingly.

In terms of promotions, the chance of receiving one usually depends largely on who upstairs likes the employee. That in turn depends as much on personality as on performance. Middle- and lower-level managers tune into who among their charge is considered a rising star. Some will give the rising star the deserved higher rating, but others will use the evaluation to neutralize a potential competitor by sowing seeds of doubt about their abilities. Still others will give a bad evaluation so as not to lose the talents of a conscientious and gifted worker. No matter what the case, the approach breeds competition when cooperation is the key to success.

The third purpose of performance evaluations, improving performance, has already been covered in Chapter 4, Is It Possibly Time for Manaagement by Objective to Bite the Dust? The focus is usually on individual accomplishments instead of the team's or the organization's as a whole; a damper is put on creativity; objectives defined during the session can become obsolete within weeks (even days).

But there is also another previously mentioned problem in terms of improved performance. I am a manager. I have 15 people reporting to me. I have a large number of responsibilities other than shepherding my reports. How exactly am I going to find the time to observe each of those 15 employees, whose jobs overlap increasingly, on an ongoing basis to evaluate their individual performance during the six months or year that the evaluation period covers? And, if I am unable to do so (an impossibility if I pay adequate attention to my other responsibilities as well), what is my evaluation going to be based on?

In terms of "private time," of using that one hour a year or every six months to improve one's relationship with one's boss, sure, why not spend the time? But if employees and managers have to depend on that one hour a year or every six months for relationship building when communication is key to success in the modern business world, something is very wrong, indeed, with the organization's management system.

Finally, in terms of documenting performance in case an employee has to be disciplined or fired, yes, the performance evaluation is of value, especially in today's world where it is so easy to take employers to court for discrimination. The performance evaluation is extremely important in this respect.

Real Criteria

Now, only one out of the five listed uses for evaluations remains valid in today's workplace. And, on top of that, any way you set up the performance evaluation, subjectivity and politics are going to influence outcomes. Employees know this. Most resent it. Some play the game and try to take advantage of the situation. In either case, a lot of time is usually wasted, especially on the part of the manager doing the evaluations; a lot of emotional energy is expended; and most important, morale cannot help but be negatively affected for at least part of the workforce.

When a progressive company becomes involved in a serious effort to improve productivity, the essential object is to take fuller advantage of employee experience and expertise on all levels and to integrate that expertise in the most effective manner. This calls for three interdependent things—a cooperative rather than competitive atmosphere where individual employees expend their energies supporting each other's efforts rather than competing against each other; a well-designed team approach; and an organization-wide, holistic perspective.

The traditional performance evaluation is antithetical to a cooperative atmosphere. It is antithetical to a team approach. It is antithetical to an organization-wide holistic perspective.

Concerning cooperation, one of the evaluation criteria in modern times is the ability to work with others. But in that the traditional reward system allows only a small percentage of the workforce to receive top-level pay increases (no matter how small the difference between levels might be) and gives only one employee the promotion, competition is unavoidable. Peers are automatically pitted against one another.

Forcing employees to focus on individual performance is dangerous in another way. The fact that an individual excels does not necessarily mean the organization as a whole does well. In fact, in a competitive or conflict-driven environment, individuals might be tempted to do well at the expense of peers. Managers, of course, are responsible for refereeing and keeping this from occurring. But managers are also forced to compete. They might be tempted to pit their reports against one another, to make them feel indebted to ensure their support. Such challenges and the resultant machinations invariably create a schizoid, highly stressful environment.

In terms of teamwork, what happens when rewards are individualized should be quite obvious. Mary and Peter are on the same team. Mary gets credit for being a good team player and is rewarded. Peter is not. Peter can do either of two things. He can quit the team and spend time sulking and telling people why team efforts really don't work, or he can begin competing against Mary to see if he can become the better team player while at the same time making her look not quite so good.

The kind of world too frequently created in workplaces with competition-driven reward systems resembles a professional basketball team where individual players are paid according to the number of points they score. The effects of such a strategy on performance are immediately obvious to sports fans. Why, then, are they not obvious to corporate executives?

In terms of the organization-wide, holistic perspective, when one is forced to focus on oneself, it is difficult to keep the big picture in mind. And when employees do begin seriously shaping their activities to benefit "the whole" rather than making "what's in it for me?" their number one priority, it is too frequently seen as a sign of vulnerability or a trick to get ahead.

To Make Matters Far Worse

How many people have worked for companies where the performance evaluation system breaks the workforce down into categories of 20 percent superior, 60 percent average, and 20 percent not up to snuff? How many know of companies where an employee who is ranked in the lowest 20 percent is in danger of losing his or her job, where employees who find themselves on this lowest level are expected to do whatever necessary to climb out of it.

This is the mythical bell-shaped density curve (BSDC) concept at work, an unproven, misused scientific hypothesis that for decades has pushed companies down the wrong path. Although the competition generated by the BSDC is meant to inspire, it has more often created a punishment-driven, strictly hierarchical culture where the focus is more on individual survival no matter what it takes, no matter who has to be sacrificed, than on thinking creatively, developing talents, and helping to improve the fortune of the company.

Historically, when owners and managers have wanted to justify a questionable approach in terms of how employees are treated, they have turned to science. Thus, the previously mentioned social Darwinists of the late 1800s and early 1900s loosely applied Charles Darwin's theory of evolution and its resultant "law of the jungle" to the workplace to excuse rampant exploitation, though they never produced or even attempted to produce the research necessary to substantiate their claims. They also failed to deal with at least one obvious weakness of their argument, which is that while in the jungle animals have to eat each other to survive, in the workplace other ways exist to accomplish these ends, ways that do not force us to take advantage of each other or to "eat" our co-workers.

The BSDC concept was adapted similarly as a rationalization for a questionable practice, that of creating competition between employees as a means of (1) keeping them under control, (2) making them dependent on their boss, and (3) keeping payroll numbers down.

According to popular belief, the BSDC concept says that when a characteristic varies in a population, it generally follows the same pattern. Most data points are similar and lie in the middle of the range. A smaller number lie at either end. Thus, for example, most men stand between the heights of 5'8" and 5'11". A smaller number taper off at heights above

5'11". A smaller number taper off at heights beneath 5'8". Thus, for example, we have decided that most of those in a workforce (60 percent) normally produce an average amount. A smaller number (20 percent) produce an above-average amount, and a smaller number (20 percent) produce a below-average amount.

Why It Doesn't Work

This logic is simple, perhaps useful; but it is also dead wrong! Several serious faults lie with this approach, faults that are keeping us from more fully realizing our potential as organizations. The first is that the BSDC concept has not been proven scientifically valid. It is not a law, not even a theory. It is a statistically based descriptive device that demonstrates a curve that population characteristic data points *sometimes* create. It is a phenomenon that is interesting to scientists, but it is not one of science's building blocks.

The BSDC was first defined in 1733 by a man named DeMoivre, then redefined a half century later by astronomers named LaPlace and Gauss, who used it to describe the behavior of errors in astronomical measurements. The curve shows up significantly only in large populations, be these populations natural, mechanical, or human. And when we say large, we mean just that. We are talking about thousands or hundreds of thousands of data points, even millions. The smaller the sample size, as all scientists know, the less chance there is of it accurately portraying the true distribution of the characteristic being defined in the population represented, even when the densities of the distribution in the sample do, in fact, create a BSDC.

Fault number one, therefore, has two parts. First, the BSDC is not a given, it is only a theory that sometimes proves true. Forcing population characteristics to fit it, therefore, is invalid scientifically and, in the workplace situation, wrong morally once we understand the error of our thinking.

Second, the BSDC materializes only when an extremely large number of data points are involved, hundreds of thousands or millions. Even if the population as a whole (all the employees in the United States lumped together, for example) does fit the curve in terms of productivity, using it to define the productivity of smaller units (offices, departments, divisions, individual companies) is invalid scientifically and, in the workplace situation, once again, wrong morally after we understand the error of our thinking.

And this brings us to serious fault number two, which is even more basic and insidious than serious fault number one. Fault number two stems from the realization that human beings are *purposeful systems* and, as such, according to Russell Ackoff and Fred Emery in their 1972 book *On Purposeful Systems,* can improve their performance if given the right incentive. Part of Ackoff and Emery's definition of a purposeful system is that it can "change its goals in a constant environment, it can define and redefine its goals, as well as the ways it pursues them" (p. 31). This is because a purposeful system has *will* and *desire*.

We all know of instances where employees and companies have redefined their goals and have improved their performance tremendously. Such turnarounds occur not because management has mandated change, but because the workforce has made a decision based on a belief that it will benefit from doing things differently.

The Way It Should Be Done

One of the companies that "gets it" is Johnsonville Sausage, located in Sheboygan Falls, Wisconsin. The owner, Ralph Stayer, has said that he believes that it is "immoral" not to do everything possible to facilitate employees' efforts to develop their potential. The company's reward system, rather than forcing people to compete for the prize, rather than making it impossible for a portion of the workforce not to lose no matter how productive they are, is organized so that everyone willing to make the effort can increase their salary. Quite simply, a series of steps has been put into place. To earn a raise, workers have to learn something new that benefits the operation—bookkeeping, quality control techniques, team leadership skills, etc. The more they learn, the more they earn, and the more, of course, the company benefits.

It's that simple.

Another important feature of the Johnsonville approach is that the employees have been given responsibility for hiring, training, and when necessary, firing team members—a change that addresses the fifth purpose of traditional performance evaluations, but more on that later.

A second company that went even further than Johnsonville Sausage was the Bridgeport Paper Company. Its parent company, Rhino Copy, was in the duplicating business. In 1990 Rhino started Bridgeport Paper in a suburb of Philadelphia to serve two purposes. The first was to function as a source of paper for Rhino. The second was to carve out a niche in the Philadelphia market for office paper supplies. The competition faced was fierce. Five other well-established companies in the area had been battling over customers for years. No populations remained untapped, no business sectors unapproached. If Bridgeport was to survive, it had to take customers away from these existing firms.

Doug Ferguson, the new president, was not a traditional manager. He had been considered somewhat of a rebel in previous jobs, frequently rocking the boat, always looking for better ways of doing things. His new staff at Bridgeport included outside sales people, inside sales people, support staff, warehouse workers, and delivery truck drivers.

Doug knew that in order to survive he needed to quickly find ways to generate a high level of commitment in these employees; ways to develop a means of taking full advantage of their expertise, many having been in the paper industry most of their careers; and ways to build a well-integrated team effort.

With these objectives in mind, the first thing the new president did was to announce that he welcomed suggestions from everybody. Almost immediately, during the hiring process, one was offered that produced good results. It was based on the observation that while a majority of the purchasing managers being contacted as potential customers were women, almost all of the outside sales people fielded by the competition were men. Bridgeport began hiring female outside sales people. Another suggestion was that Bridgeport should provide 24-hour service, as the competition delivered only during the day.

After the staff had been hired, Doug called a meeting with everybody and announced that he was making the new employees responsible for designing key organization systems—communication, access to information, decision making, work design, training, recruiting, evaluation, reward, and discipline. It took more than an hour for Doug to convince his staff that he was serious, that they, indeed, had been given the authority to do so without fear of repercussion.

Eventually, a hand went up. One of the inside sales people, obviously nervous, stood and said tentatively that if he was truly being asked for his opinion, he would like to address the reward system. Doug replied, "Fine." The man then complained that while outside sales people traditionally worked on a commission basis, inside sales people were salaried. This was not fair because, while outside sales earned a great deal of money for establishing contact and giving the initial pitch, inside sales earned a lot less, even though, after taking over, they frequently made the sale or at least completed it. He thought that the commission should be divided in some manner.

The staff then discussed this suggestion and though some outside sales people disagreed and two eventually quit, it was decided that dividing the commission was a good idea. After reaching the agreement, the employees looked to Doug for his decision or objections. He just shook his head and said quietly,

"You are designing the systems, not me. If you think this is a good idea, we'll try it. If it works, fine. If we run into problems, we'll change it."

Next, a support staff person stood up and said that, yes, the outside and inside sales people made the sale, but if support staff failed to do its job, taking calls from customers, scheduling, answering questions, reassuring, fielding complaints, a lot of the deals would fall through. She believed that support staff deserved part of the commission as well. Again, the group discussed this idea and decided that it made sense.

The next person to speak was a warehouse worker. He argued that while outside and inside sales people managed the sale with support staff tending to details, if the people in his area didn't handle their responsibilities correctly, both individual sales and customers could be lost. Warehouse employees deserved a share of the commission as well.

Then, a delivery truck driver stood up and said basically the same thing.

Coming Up with Something New

After much debate, the result of this initial effort was what the employees considered a unique team approach to sales. Teams, rather than individual outside sales people, would be given territories to work. Each team would consist of outside sales, inside sales, support staff, somebody in the warehouse to oversee loading, and a delivery truck driver or drivers.

A three-tiered reward system for these teams was eventually put into place. On the lowest level the company instituted a salary for all employees. The salary was minimal except for top-level managers, who were not part of a sales team. Salary raises would be based on the number of years served, rather than on productivity, and would be relatively small. The next level would be the team commission, comprised of a percentage of each team's sales revenues. This commission would be divided among team members according to a formula worked out during the staff exercise and monitored afterward by a committee including representatives from each function. The third level would include a bonus, another percentage of each sale made by each team being put into a common pot to be divided among employees every four months.

When the issue of how the bonus money should be divided, who should get what percentage, was introduced, several employees spoke about working for corporations where upper-level executives received hundreds of thousands of dollars in bonus money while lower-level employees were lucky to come away with a thousand. They had found that insulting. The decision was finally made that everybody in the company, from Doug on down, should be awarded the same amount.

It was then agreed that the percentage of profits that went into team commissions and the percentage that went into the corporate bonus should eventually be adjusted to ensure that the amount earned through the bonus was larger than that earned from team commissions. This was done to discourage competition between teams, to encourage them to share information and other resources. The logic behind this move was, the more my team cooperates with your team, the more we support your efforts and you support ours, the larger my bonus, the larger my paycheck is going to be.

With this reward system in place, one that truly empowered employees, one that encouraged and rewarded cooperation, the new workforce went on to suggest that the teams be made responsible for their own recruiting, training, and discipline. Team members knew better than anyone what they needed when it came time to hire staff replacements or additional staff. At the same time, it was obvious that because individual teams had no manager or leader, they should be responsible for communication and decision making at the level most important to them.

Finally, the suggestion was also made that representatives of the individual teams meet weekly to further integrate efforts and that someone from upper-level management should attend these meetings.

A World without Performance Evaluations

The last issue addressed was employee evaluations. The nervousness that had been there when the workforce first met returned. This was obviously not a popular topic. The different approaches were discussed—boss evaluating employees using MBO, employees evaluating boss, the two evaluating each other, self-evaluations, peer evaluations, 360-degree evaluations. None seemed to fit the new arrangement comfortably. Most of those coming from other jobs in the industry were familiar with MBO, but due to its emphasis on the individual and its restrictive nature in terms of setting pre-defining objectives and also the additional time it took that employees thought could be better spent selling paper, very few wanted it.

The suggestion was made that MBO might be applied to teams rather than individuals. This seemed a possibility, but again the employees saw it mainly as a waste of time. Team objectives were clearly defined and simple. The role that team members played might change daily or even hourly. The important thing was for them to remain as flexible as possible to take advantage of unexpected opportunities.

Then, Doug, who had only answered questions up to this point, letting the employees carry the discussion, spoke. "This has all been very interesting," he said. "But I've been thinking. We have all worked hard to design a reward system that encourages cooperation; that encourages teams as well as individuals to communicate and share information, to facilitate each other's efforts in any way possible. We don't have to worry about who gets raises with this system. Salaries, hopefully, will not provide the major part of our income. If we leave promotion decisions up to the workforce I imagine you will pick the people who you believe can benefit us all the most. With this system in place, discipline issues will be addressed by teams rather than by managers, greatly reducing the possibility of the company being taken to court for discrimination. Teams will be in charge of training their members as well as hiring new members. …We have defined our objectives collectively; but we are not locked into them. We can and will change them anytime we agree that a different way is better." He hesitated, "…With all this in mind, I have no doubt that we will be evaluating ourselves and each other informally on a continual basis, that we will constantly be trying to increase our individual productivity as well as that of our peers, our team, the team network, those of us in administrative positions, and finally the productivity of the company as a whole." Doug hesitated again. Then he shrugged and smiled, "…So, what's left?"

As a result of those meetings, Bridgeport Paper decided to see if the company could function without MBO or any sort of formal evaluation process. The pressure, so to speak, was off from the start. Emphasis was no longer on achieving predefined objectives in order to fulfill a contract with management. Emphasis was now on selling paper and improving the bottom line to enhance everybody's income.

After this evaluation and reward system was instituted, members of the workforce continued suggesting improvements without any sort of suggestion system being put into place, without any formal reward being offered. The reward, of course, was a bottom-line improvement that everyone benefited from.

In a relatively short period of time the company began showing a profit.

If There Is a Better Way, Why, Then…

Keeping one's job has been the traditional incentive to improving one's performance; but it is no longer the only necessary one or even, in most instances, the most important one. Making more money has also been an incentive. But again, it is no longer the most important after a reasonable level of income is reached. The most important modern industrial-world incentive to improved performance has proven time and again to be respect—that management respect my needs and desires as an employee and as an individual, that management respect my potential, my ideas. The companies that have done the best, quite simply, are those that have shown the most respect for employee potential, that have encouraged employees to contribute to the fullest possible extent according to their expertise, that have encouraged employees to work together as a team and have rewarded them accordingly, rather than pitting them against each other.

These companies have understood the very simple fact that management's objective should be to help every employee become part of the most productive 20 percent. They have understood that insisting on a bell-shaped curve in terms of employee productivity is, in fact, counterproductive when dealing with a workforce capable of constant improvement. They have understood that the best results are generated when employees are supporting each other's efforts. They have understood that in such situations management *facilitation* rather than management *control* is the key to success.

The question, of course, is, *Can other companies adopt a model similar to the one put into place at Johnsonville Sausage or at Bridgeport Paper?* The answer I would offer is, *Why not?* Nothing suggested in this chapter is new. It has all been out there for some time now. It has proven its value over and over. But most companies continue to refuse to pay attention; most companies stubbornly stick to the old ways, no matter how overwhelming the proof might be.

At this point, then, organizations have a choice. They can continue trying to preserve the old culture, or they can move on. If they choose the latter course and begin building a new

culture, the place they must start is with the performance evaluation and the reward systems, for these two systems, more
than any other, shape our workplace culture. Until organizations accept the need for change in these systems, the rest of
the desired improvements, no matter how hard they try, will
continue to lie beyond their reach.

Chapter 6

Doing It Wrong: Or, How Can Quality Improvement Efforts Possibly Get So Screwed Up?

One of the follow-up questions we must ask at this point is, What steps should we take once management decides that a cooperative environment is more beneficial than one that generates competition or conflict, once management puts into place an evaluation and reward system that encourages the desired cooperation? This can be further broken down into the following questions: How should we organize or reorganize our management systems so that they support the desired change? How do we get things done; how do we accomplish our objectives in this new world? Will the traditional management hierarchy still work? Will it allow the company to make use of employee expertise? Will it allow employees to contribute in the way that they can and should? Or do we need something new; do we need to design a new way to make decisions, to gather and make effective use of the information on which improvements are based?

A vehicle already exists that can facilitate the necessary changes. But this will occur only if the effort is designed and implemented in the correct manner. The vehicle was first introduced as part of the quality improvement movement that started in the United States when we realized that other nations were cutting into world markets we had dominated for years by stressing *quality* in their products while we continued to focus on *quantity,* on getting the product out the door as quickly as possible.

Quality improvement became the buzzword. The federal government even created the Baldrige National Quality Award to encourage this national trend. The problem was, however, that very few organizations had any real idea of what was needed, or when told what was needed, handpicked the parts they felt comfortable with and ignored the rest.

Dr. Deming's previously mentioned work is a prime example of this latter phenomenon. At the same time, thousands of expensive consultants sporting well-designed sales pitches piled in. These consultants, for the most part, offered canned approaches that focused on one part of what was required—on the introduction of statistical measurement tools, on team building, on creating a "zero defects" environment, on employing conflict management, on stimulating creativity, on suggestion systems—while not paying much attention to the rest and to the required interactions..

The result of all this confusion, all this misinformation, all this lack of comprehensiveness and lack of perspective, was too frequently disappointment and cynicism when a year later the companies discovered that they had very little if any bottom-line improvement to show for the thousands of dollars spent. As a result, the quality movement is now seen by most as another fad whose time has passed…which is a real shame.

Quality improvement cannot be a passing fad if the United States is to remain competitive in the world marketplace. It must become a permanent part of every organization's agenda. If the desired results are to be achieved, however, things have to be done right. Quality improvement efforts have to be built on foundational changes in the organization's culture, many of these changes being the ones discussed in previous chapters.

Off to a Bad Start

Let's discuss a real-world case study to show what happens when organizations "talk the talk" in terms of increased productivity and an improved long-term bottom line but are unwilling or unable to "walk the talk" once the ramifications of what is necessary become obvious. In this case study we shall discuss a company that did almost everything wrong. We shall talk about why the process began, the steps taken, and why these steps did not produce the desired results.

The organization we shall focus on is in the insurance industry. We shall call it Company X. Quality improvement was introduced at Company X by the executive board after a reengineering project complete with the usual downsizing ended up hurting the bottom line rather than helping it.

Reengineering has been discussed in Chapter 1. It was a concept originally developed by Henry Ford to improve technical manufacturing systems and products, and was reintroduced in recent years as a means of making the workforce in combination with technology, more efficient. Unfortunately, in too many cases reengineering has become simply another excuse for cutting jobs as a means of improving the short-term bottom line. When a quality improvement process is introduced in an attempt to clean up the mess after a misguided reengineering effort, employees are naturally suspicious of upper-level management's motives. The key ingredient to success—employee commitment—is much harder to achieve. If Company X had begun with a comprehensive quality improvement process instead, and had involved the employees on all levels in efforts to improve the operation, greater efficiencies would have been realized in a wider range of areas with fewer negative consequences and, perhaps, without the need to introduce reengineering.

After the quality improvement process was introduced to top-level management by the board of directors, division vice presidents were made responsible for presenting it to their units and for getting things started. They were told that their degree of success in doing so would affect their performance evaluation. How the vice presidents organized the effort was left up to them individually.

Immediately, Company X introduced three elements that are antithetical to a successful quality improvement process. The first was "top-downism." Executive management, rather than convincing the division vice presidents that supporting the process would benefit themselves as well as the company said, in effect, "You *will* get involved! We're holding your performance evaluation as a club over your head to make sure that you do." All people react best to a logical explanation delivered in a respectful manner, especially one that includes a definition of the benefits to themselves. At the same time, all people resent being threatened, no matter how subtle the threat, and tend to resist.

The second antithetical element introduced was competition. Top management immediately pitted the vice presidents against each other by adding their level of successful involvement in the quality process to the already competitive performance evaluation criteria. The competitive environment was then further intensified by the fact that, instead of encouraging the vice presidents to work together to come up with an approach, how each vice president got things started, how each introduced the effort and shaped it in his or her individual division was left to that person's discretion.

The third antithetical element introduced was fragmentation. Two things that bind successful quality improvement processes together, that allow the necessary integration of efforts going on all over the organization, are a common language and communication. When each unit is doing its own thing, the necessary common language does not exist. Also, because of the competitive environment, communication between units tends to decrease rather than increase. Even if one division's effort is highly successful, therefore, its effects on the organization as a whole might be negative.

Going the Individualized Route

In at least one division, the Claims Division, the first step taken was to bring a consultant in to assess employee attitudes and employee perceptions concerning division performance. Focus groups were formed and members surveyed for opinions.

Two different approaches to quality improvement are the *individual-oriented* approach and the *systems-oriented* approach. The individual-oriented approach focuses initially on the individual employee, tries to discover what he or she is feeling, what and who the employee thinks is the problem, usually through a survey of some sort. The information gathered from individuals is then consolidated, studied, fed back, and discussed. Eventually, key issues are defined and task forces are formed to deal with them.

The systems-oriented approach focuses instead on organization systems. It believes that if the communication, access to information, problem solving and decision making, work design, training, evaluation and reward systems are made to function more effectively, most of the people problems will disappear. Rather than first surveying employees to gather information for top-level management and consultants to analyze, therefore, the systems approach (the International Paper Company project described in Chapter 2 is one example) immediately gives employees on all levels the authority to identify, design, and implement process-related improvement in their own areas of expertise. The individual obviously remains a key player in this scenario, but the focus is on the *system* rather than on the *isolated employee*. Also, while the individual approach (the survey) is, once again, something *done to* the employee, orchestrated and controlled by top management, with the systems approach the employee is given control; the employee is truly, rather than superficially, empowered.

The results of this survey were given to division top-level management, which announced that after a thorough review the results would be released to the workforce. What happened, in fact, was that only a carefully edited version of survey results was fed back to the contributors, containing what many considered to be severe distortions of what had been said.

So much for trust. So much for any serious attempt by the workforce to make improvements. Any commitment to the process that might have been generated up to this point was now gone. Management obviously had its own agenda. From that point on, the employees would do and say as little as possible and only things they thought were expected.

The Rock and the Hard Place

An advisory group was formed to pick three issues out of the pages generated by the survey. These issues were then passed on to a Continuous Improvement Committee (CIC) including representatives from all levels to be worked on. The CIC was charged with getting input from those represented and with then making recommendations to the Division Lead Team composed of the vice president and upper-level managers concerning how to deal with the issues involved. After the Lead Team took these recommendations into account and decided what course of action to follow, the CIC was responsible for communicating the Lead Team's decisions to lower levels and supporting them.

The CIC was initially told that it would be responsible for identifying possible improvements in the company's approach to indemnity and expense management, customer service, and employee development. Obviously, the range of possible interests gleaned from the survey had been narrowed considerably by the advisory group. It was also made clear to the CIC that employee development projects were to come last on the list.

This is a mainly top-down approach. A CIC was formed and initially given broad parameters in terms of what it could work on. Very quickly, however, these parameters were narrowed, both by limiting the number of projects to be addressed and by indicating that employee-development-related projects were not a priority. Also, the CIC was made responsible only for offering recommendations to the Lead Team.

The vice president of the Home Office Claims Division also made it clear that he expected quick results from the task forces formed to deal with each of the three issues selected, as though their efforts should not interfere with their normal workload.

The final blow to the process came when the vice president of Claims said, "Your normal responsibilities cannot be allowed to suffer," and "I need quick results." He was showing his willingness to sacrifice the employees' quality of working life in order to achieve the desired results. Such actions do not demonstrate the respect that is, as we have said, a critical ingredient to successful quality improvement processes. Emphasis remained on making management look good, rather than on making the workforce as a whole look good.

All employees in Company X were required to attend training sessions. Attendance was monitored and impacted employee performance evaluations. One division had only two trainers for almost a thousand employees spread over a large region. Scheduling the training sessions in this situation was, of course, a major problem. Also, the training was, again, piled on top of their normal workload so that the employees resented it.

Training is an important part of any comprehensive quality improvement effort. The way that it is carried out in most instances, however, is largely a waste of both employee time and company money. Two types of training are involved. The first concerns how to participate in the quality improvement effort itself. This includes training in teamwork, facilitation, problem identification and solution, and conflict resolution. The second type is job-related training. This includes improvements in such things as customer service, the use of computers, the use of machinery, file keeping, and management practices. Company X insisted that everyone participate in quality process training up front so that employees could function more effectively in team efforts. The implication was that adult staff members—most of whom have been employed for a number of years—did not know how to work together effectively, did not know how to identify and solve problems, or how to resolve conflict. The systems approach believes that employees already know what the problems are and simply need an opportunity to identify and work on them. Team problem-solving efforts in a systemic process, therefore, begin immediately without months of preparatory training.

What was to be covered in terms of job-related training at Company X was, once again, defined by management. As part of a systemic approach to quality improvement, a majority of such training needs, as we have said, are identified by the employees themselves.

Planning as a Threat

Organization-wide planning at Company X included the identification of objectives by executives and the generation of wish lists by lower-level managers. During this part of the process, employees were reminded that planning efforts produced work and that those who identified projects would most likely be held responsible for their completion.

Effective long-range planning is necessary to any successful quality improvement process. It provides a frame of reference for team problem-solving and design efforts. It defines the overall objectives that team projects must complement. Long-range planning cannot be done alongside a quality improvement process. It must, instead, be a well-integrated part of such processes. Employees must understand and be committed to the organization's objectives defined. The best way to develop such understanding and commitment is to encourage employees on all levels to contribute to the definition of these objectives. Such a contribution can be made through team efforts. While the long-range objectives defined by senior management provide a frame of reference for team projects, the projects defined and pursued by teams increasingly affect the nature of the long-range objectives identified.

A wish list like the one passed up through the levels at Company X is the workforce going to top management with hat in hand saying, "Please, sir, more porridge." The wish list approach does not help employees understand the organization's long-range objectives. It does not help units understand each other's operations and how they must fit together. It is antithetical to integration. It encourages competition for resources rather than the cooperation required for a quality improvement process to be successful.

A Little Dab of Intrigue to Spice Things Up

As part of the exercise, employees were asked to complete feedback forms as a means of critiquing the process-related performance of peers.

Peer evaluations are frequently a cornerstone of the individual-oriented approach to quality improvement. Their value is that they sometimes help employees understand each other better, that they help clear the air. More frequently, however, they have a negative effect. They breed uncertainty, suspicion, competition, and sometimes anger. By instituting the peer evaluation approach, Company X further fragmented the process by focusing it on individual performance rather than on the creation of an atmosphere that encouraged cooperation and teamwork.

Vice presidents and other managers were frequently reticent to act on employee suggestions.

Due to the top-down culture found in Company X, due to the highly competitive atmosphere generated among managers, a question of great concern was, Why didn't I think of this before my workers did? The competitive atmosphere choked process improvement rather than fostered it, because managers would think, When those working for me identify problems with the way we are currently doing things, it makes me look bad in front of my boss; therefore, it is safer to just smother their suggestions.

There is little reason to be surprised by the fact that the quality improvement process quickly faded at Company X. The reason given was that the workers on lower levels didn't seem to comprehend its importance to the company and to their own situation. Management complained that the workers wanted to concentrate on work environment issues first, issues that should be resolved elsewhere, not as part of the quality improvement process. Eventually, some of the people responsible for putting the process into place were fired.

A fitting, though sad, ending followed. Top-level management set the process up for failure by refusing to empower those responsible for producing results. Then top-level management scapegoated them. The fact that workers wanted to deal first with work environment issues—a lack of glare screens, drafts, a lack of filing cabinet space, telephones that didn't work, uncomfortable desk chairs—is totally logical in that these issues had the most immediate effect on individual performance. Even if management was shortsighted enough to consider such issues irrelevant, allowing the CIC members to begin by picking and working on the things most important to themselves would have sent the signal that bosses were taking into account the needs of the workforce as well as their own.

In this case, management obviously didn't send that signal. As a result, in the future, when it comes time for the next attempt to improve quality at Company X to start, getting lower-level employees involved will be even more difficult.

Unfortunately, this scenario has been repeated, with variations, time and again at a wide range of companies. The best we can hope for is that it will serve as a learning experience and that the next time around, management's new understanding will allow a greater degree of success.

Chapter 7

Doing It Right: Or, Moving Beyond the Baldrige

When modern-day companies talk about change, they frequently mean fine-tuning their current cultures, introducing quantitative tools and nonquantitative techniques to make the operation increasingly efficient, eventually to the point of maximum return. But then these companies begin to spin their wheels because productivity hasn't reached the desired level and because they don't know what to do next. Frustration replaces previous feelings of achievement. The companies find themselves trapped in a dilemma, a problematic situation that cannot be resolved in its current context.

The context we are referring to in this situation is the organization's culture. *Efficiency*-enhancing efforts have to do with getting the most out of the current culture, rather than with changing it. *Effectiveness*-enhancing efforts, on the other hand, have to do with making change in the culture necessary to improved performance in all sectors and on all levels.

Organizations frequently find the changes required for them to shift their focus toward effectiveness too threatening and therefore never get beyond the increased efficiency orientation. But more and more organizations are beginning to understand that the traditional business model, with its focus solely on efficiencies, is not producing the results that it used to. A shift toward effectiveness is rapidly becoming requisite to survival, much less success.

Any change effort has three stages—design, implementation, and feedback/further modification. In boss-driven efforts the design stage usually progresses relatively rapidly; it is much easier for one person to make all the decisions than to integrate the ideas of a large number of employees, though the results are rarely as rich or as well thought out. The implementation stage, however, is when the team effort catches up and pulls away. When employees have contributed to an improvement, they understand it; they have gained "ownership" so that they will strive to make implementation successful. When it's the boss's idea, employees tend to either leave it up to the boss or to do exactly what they are told without question, even though they see problems looming.

In terms of feedback/further improvements, it's a lot easier to discover weaknesses and to make improvements in a team-driven project because there is more than one set of eyes keeping watch, there is more than just one brain coming up with suggestions concerning further modifications.

As we have already said and demonstrated several times in the book, the most valuable resource any organization has in terms of improving performance is its employee's expertise and commitment. So, now, it is time to talk about how to design and orchestrate organization change in a way that will make the most effective use of that expertise and commitment.

The Ideal: What We Need to Aim For

Most quality improvement processes are not producing the desired results. The reason is that they lack critical characteristics or pieces. This is frequently because those shaping the process do not yet understand. They do not understand that what is going on today in serious quality improvement efforts is simply the latest version of the Systems approach, which was introduced in Chapter 1.

The Systems approach to management, organization design, and planning is based on the realization that "the whole is more than the sum of its parts." Interactions between an organization's parts create characteristics that none of the parts possess individually, characteristics critical to the identity of the whole. When some of the parts are excluded from organization processes, or are not properly utilized, the whole (the organization) cannot function in the most effective manner.

In terms of quality improvement, the "part" we must pay most attention to is the employee. Without effectively cultivating and utilizing our employees' expertise, we will not get the most out of our technology, no matter how efficient it is; we will not meet organization objectives; we will not play the role we wish to play in the marketplace and in society. The employee, not technology, not the customer, drives such improvement processes. Also, because a whole is more than the sum of its parts, employee efforts must be well integrated and ongoing.

Finally, in order to make employees more effective, there must be constant feedback and an opportunity for continual learning (sound familiar?). The continual learning serves two purposes. First, it makes employees more effective in their efforts to improve products, manufacturing/service delivery processes, management systems, and the work environment. Second, it helps to satisfy one of the greatest needs that employees have in relation to self-development: increased control over their work life.

Such increased control for employees is critical as well to development of the organization as a whole. The process of giving this control is called *empowerment*. We all know this term; it has been making the rounds for some time now.

Without empowerment nothing else bears fruit: neither our attempt to gain commitment, nor our enhanced training schedule, nor our better integrated planning effort.

Empowerment is the key to successful quality improvement. Managers attend seminars on empowerment. They watch films on empowerment. They even visit successful organizations to take home ideas on how to empower their workforce. They listen carefully and take notes. But what they miss, what they fail to carry back in their notebooks, probably because it's too far out of sync with their current reality, is the need to empower the workforce *fully* and the explanation of what that means.

"Wait just one minute," goes the refrain. "We empower our employees! We train them in team dynamics. We have suggestion systems. We put them on teams and let them work on important issues. And when the work is completed, everyone involved is thanked, congratulated, and rewarded—not just the managers."

Partial Empowerment Just Doesn't Cut It

Any organization seriously committed to quality improvement believes it has made an effort to empower its employees and probably will defend that effort. The problem, however, is one of *degree*, not of *intention*. Those guiding a majority of current organization improvement efforts quite possibly have confused *partial* empowerment with *full* empowerment, and the latter is quite different. The problem is that partial empowerment generates only partial commitment in employees and produces, at best, only partial success.

When we partially empower employees, we treat them like adolescents rather than like grown-ups, and that is a costly mistake. As parents, when our offspring reach adolescence, we no longer want to treat them as children; we no longer want simply to tell them what to do. Rather, we want them to begin exercising their own judgment, to begin making at least some of their own decisions. However, owing to their lack of experience we, as parents, reserve the right to overrule. We continue to set policy. Ultimately, we are still in charge. And we make sure that our kids understand this, because we are not quite ready to cut them loose.

This is the way most managers treat employees. They want employees' input. They want employees to begin contributing to decisions. But most managers also want to make sure the employee understands that the manager is still in charge.

In the workplace, however, most employees are not adolescents. They are adults, just like managers, and function best when treated as such. As adults they spend the majority of their waking hours solving problems, making decisions, handling family finances, settling disputes, managing projects, working as equals with others to improve the community, doing all the things that normal adults do, taking all the responsibilities that normal adults take. Yet in too many organizations, each time they pass through the office or shop door, employees are forced to regress to adolescence. They are expected to ask their boss to help solve problems they would normally have no difficulty solving themselves. They may not be allowed to communicate directly with one another and often are not allowed to make even minor decisions.

In summary, the concept of *full empowerment* needs to be understood if we are to make effective use of an organization's most valuable resource, its employees' expertise, to improve quality. Partial doesn't cut it. And the best way to encourage full empowerment is to begin thinking systemically.

Putting All the Things Together into a Model That Works

Most quality improvement process models include some of the characteristics required for success or have all of the characteristics in varying degrees. Only one that we are familiar with, however, possesses them all to the necessary degree. It should come as no surprise that the model we are talking about is called the Systems model. After laying out the basics of the Systems model for quality improvement, we shall proceed to discuss two other models that have enjoyed popularity—the Philip Crosby model and the Malcolm Baldrige National Quality Award model—identifying their strengths and weaknesses from a systems perspective.

The Systems model includes five phases: familiarization, team building, group process skills learning, the introduction of process definition and statistical measurement techniques when appropriate, and long-range planning. The five phases of the Systems model are considered to be highly *interdependent*. They must complement and support each other. The most important of these phases is team building. This phase leads the way, providing the necessary structure and generating the culture upon which the success of the others depends.

The Systems model starts with *familiarization*, a brief introduction of process objectives and of the approach to be used to achieve these objectives. *It then moves directly into team building rather than into process-related training*. The logic behind this nontraditional decision is threefold: First, process-related training should be conducted on-the-job during the team-building phase rather than before it in order to be most effective. Second, in order to succeed, a quality improvement process must provide two things initially. One is a sense of participant ownership. This cannot be delivered through training. It is only achieved through team-related activities and learning. The other thing required is quick results. The investment necessary to start a quality improvement process is relatively large, at least in terms of time. Organization leaders quickly begin getting nervous when they have to wait to see results. Third, employees are skeptical about management's claim that they are being empowered. This skepticism is allayed only when they begin completing team-controlled projects.

The Systems model depends on three types of teams. The first type includes improvement-focused teams (hourly problem-solving teams, managerial design teams). These teams represent different functions and span the organization. We talk about them representing functions instead of departments for a specific reason. Secretaries and maintenance workers represent "functions" that serve many departments. Instead of being made part of departmental teams, therefore, these people should begin with one of their own to deal with issues unique to their function.

Hourly workers and managers are put on different teams to ensure the empowerment of the hourly workers, the rationale being that if a manager sat on an hourly team, the hourly employees would look to that person for final decisions and would not be completely open about their concerns. Improvement teams identify the projects they want to work on, design the desired improvements, and are responsible to implement these improvements and make necessary adjustments. Improvement teams have no leader, only a facilitator from a different function. The facilitator's responsibilities include asking a lot of project-related questions, helping deal with personality issues, helping integrate team efforts with those of other teams in the network, and making sure that the process "ground rules" are followed.

Ground Rules as the Catalyst

Systemic ground rules are critical to the success of any systemic quality improvement process. They include the following:

1. Hourly team projects cannot be taken over by managers.
2. All team decisions are made by consensus.
3. Team members are not allowed to complain about a situation unless they are able to suggest a reasonable way to improve it.

4. Team members have access to all company personnel to meet their information needs.
5. Team-suggested improvement must be justified by a cost-benefit analysis when possible or a quality of working life rationale when not possible.
6. Quality improvement projects that might influence other parts of the operation must be agreed to by anyone else affected. Such stakeholders must also have a chance to contribute before implementation occurs.
7. Response to a team question must be received within one week. The response to suggestions can be, *Yes, go ahead with it*; or *No, and this is why*, with a reasonable explanation; or *Let's talk about it*, with a date set. (This is to keep threatened managers from passively killing the process.)
8. When a ground rule is violated, the team facilitator will meet with the violator for resolution. If the problem is not overcome, the facilitator will report the violation to the head facilitator, who coordinates the facilitator network. If the head facilitator cannot resolve the issue, he or she will carry it directly to top-level management for resolution.

Ground rules 4 and 6 help to ensure that managers have input into hourly problem-solving team projects, but on an as-needed basis. While hourly problem-solving teams usually work on things like how to improve a specific service or manufacturing process, managerial design projects generally take a wider scope and address things like scheduling or which services should be offered.

The second type of team is the Lead Team composed of the organization head, his or her direct reports, the improvement process head facilitator, and anyone else considered necessary. The Lead Team is responsible for facilitating the long-range planning effort that produces the framework of overall organization objectives into which team projects must fit. Lead Team members also contribute to hourly problem-solving team and managerial design team projects that involve a large expense or that affect organization policy. They also help integrate the effort at the highest level.

The third type of team is the task force. Any manager can form a task force around any project desired, so long as one of the improvement teams in the network is not already working on it. Task forces can include any employee considered important to the project, management or hourly. Task forces usually have a leader and offer their recommendations to the manager who forms them, rather than taking responsibility for implementation. While quality teams are ongoing, task forces dissolve once the involved project is completed.

Learning in the Systems model, as we have said, occurs on the job for both facilitators and team members. If facilitators feel they need more process-related training for themselves than is gained on the job, they can design their own sessions. In terms of work-related learning, team members identify what they believe is needed, design the sessions, and are responsible for either delivering the package themselves or finding a resource with the right skills, often with the help of the human relations function. Team facilitators eventually learn statistical measurement techniques so that when a specific technique might be helpful to a team project, they can offer it.

In terms of the required characteristics referred to earlier, the Systems model for quality improvement is obviously *participative*. Hourly workers/professionals have their own teams, identify the issues they want to work on, and are responsible for implementing as well as designing the desired changes. At the same time, due to the stakeholder involvement ground rule, managers must be allowed to contribute their input to hourly team projects. At the same time, managers have their own teams, where they can identify and work on projects *they* think important.

The Systems model is built around an organization-wide network of teams that is *integrated* by both the ground rules and the facilitators. These teams are *ongoing*. That is, they remain in place until the ground rules have been absorbed into the organization's culture and projects are identified and addressed effectively on the job rather than during team meetings.

The Systems model provides *constant feedback* and the opportunity for *continual learning*. The ground rules, again, help to ensure this. Teams have access to anyone they want for information. Teams are responsible for doing project cost-benefit analysis. Also, team members are empowered to identify their own educational needs. Finally, the planning phase is designed so that members of the organization get to contribute to the definition of overall objectives and priorities, an important part of understanding their role in the organization.

Now That We've Talked about What Should Happen, Let's Talk about What Really Happens

The Systems approach to quality improvement is not that difficult to understand or to implement. The organizations that have done so to improve productivity and the bottom line have been universally successful. The problem is that during the quality improvement movement, which was our first really big chance at cultural change, most organizations chose another approach and things did not work out as well.

Why did they choose another approach? One reason was the fear of change that is a central theme of this book. Another reason was, quite simply, ignorance. A serious focus on quality was something new. The person designated head of the new quality improvement department might know something about statistical measurement techniques or team building, but usually lacked a comprehensive background and had to learn as he or she designed the approach, while at the same time being under a great deal of pressure to begin producing positive results.

When one finds oneself in that situation, the normal thing to do is to seek outside help, which is what most new quality

improvement department heads did. And the help material-
ized almost spontaneously. Existing consulting firms suddenly
sprouted experts. Hundreds of new consulting firms material-
ized with well-crafted, well-merchandized packages to offer,
with their up-front salespeople flying all over the country
presenting glossy sales pitches complete with all the bells and
whistles to those desperately in need of a savior.

The problem was that the people making the pitch frequently possessed little more understanding of what comprehensive organization improvement entails than those being
pitched to. As a result of all this ignorance on both sides of
the table, the key to making the sale too often became the
ability to throw in the most buzzwords.

Crosby Gives Them What They Want

Philip Crosby probably made more money than any other
consultant off the quality improvement movement. His organization's approach to selling its model was masterful. When
Crosby gained a customer, he would charge a whole lot up
front, then bring upper-level management and those responsible for running the process to his "school." Next, he would
flood the organization with "experts" who would lead seminars that all employees were required to attend. The seminars
consisted of lectures, training sessions, group discussions, and
team-building exercises. Then the experts would leave, and
those who had attended the seminars were expected to return
to their units and put into place what they had learned.

When questions arose during the implementation phase,
employees could call Crosby's company, but if they needed
additional training, well, that would cost a couple more bucks,
and then a couple more bucks, and then a couple more bucks.
Within a short period of time so much had been spent that
those responsible for picking the consultant weren't about
to admit that the approach had produced very few positive

results. How could that be possible when so much training had been done? And when asked by other companies for a reference, they weren't about to say, "The money we spent was largely wasted."

To get a little more specific in terms of package content, quality improvement according to the Crosby model is a management-driven process that requires long-term commitment, not only from management but from all organization employees. The Crosby model is built on two themes. The first is that all work is a process. Every job performed is a series of actions that produce a result that must be defined in terms of customer expectation. The second theme includes Crosby's *four absolutes of quality* necessary to operating, managing, and improving production processes.

Crosby's *first absolute* defined quality as conformance to requirements and used a detailed worksheet to document these requirements. The *second absolute* emphasized preventing problems from occurring. *The third absolute* adopted zero defects as the standard that employees should aim for. The *fourth absolute* stated that the measurement for success in quality improvement efforts is the price of nonconformance, or what it costs to do things wrong compared with what it costs to do them right.

During the previously mentioned seminars, then, the first phase involved the teaching of Crosby's four absolutes. This training lasted several hours and included sessions on managing quality, teamwork, problem analysis, and the use of statistical measurement techniques. It began with top management attending a week-long course at the Crosby Quality College. Next, those chosen to be process facilitators spent two weeks at the college learning the necessary skills. Then an introductory session was given by top management to the entire workforce. More training followed. Finally, the newly trained facilitators were made responsible for leading classes on the Crosby Quality Education System that every employee attended.

Only after the completion of the education sessions did individuals and departments begin working on improvement projects. They did so by mapping out process requirements (flow diagrams). The Crosby model insisted that all team members use a specific language and a specific set of tools to complete this task. Management was responsible for identifying the organization process each group worked on. Meeting mechanics and rules of meeting etiquette were spelled out. No real attempt was made to integrate the process improvement efforts going on all over the organization. A long-range plan including a well-defined organization objective that might provide a frame of reference for team efforts was not considered a necessity.

Should We Call This Success?

The Crosby model was popular largely because it gave a lot of top-level executives exactly what they wanted. A large amount of money was spent for a whole new set of buzzwords, for tons of training that introduced very little if anything that was new. But most importantly, the traditional top-down, hierarchical management system was in no way affected. In fact, it was strengthened in the name of quality improvement. Crosby proclaimed openly that he did not believe in employee empowerment, that managers should make the decisions (which they continued to do all during the process). In this model, although employees could make suggestions, their main role was to do as they were told, to strive to meet the performance standards and requirements defined for them by management, and even to follow the rules of meeting etiquette spelled out for them.

Basically, the Crosby model, in terms of utilizing employee expertise, was a throwback to Frederick Taylor's Scientific Management. Make all the important decisions for your employees—have them leave their brains at the door and focus on doing what they are instructed to do.

Other weaknesses of the Crosby model from a Systems perspective include the fact that training was up front and was *done to* employees in the classroom, giving them no opportunity to learn on the job where things are real and where the important questions come up. Another weakness would be his third absolute, "striving for zero defects," the alternative in this case being to strive for continual improvement. Another weakness of this approach from a Systems perspective was the lack of an organization-wide improvement team network complete with ground rules as a source of empowerment, integration, and process continuity. The "teams" in Crosby's model are what we have called task forces—project specific, management driven, formed only to make suggestions, disbanded when their task is completed. Another weakness was the focus on customers rather than on employees as the most important stakeholder. Another would be the lack of long-range planning, an absolute necessity if companies want to design a well-understood whole. And finally, the Crosby model lacked integration at the lower levels. Teams frequently did not know what other teams were working on or why they had been given a specific project in terms of the big picture.

A whole lot of new buzzwords, as we said, a whole lot of motion and money spent, but very little that was new, that was different. A year or so after the dust settled and reality set back in, it was difficult to find companies that had spent all this money and dedicated all this time still paying attention to their detailed worksheets or to any of Crosby's other *absolutes of quality.*

The Baldrige: A Good Starting Point, but Still Not Biting the Bullet

The standard for quality improvement that remained when most consultant packages had fallen by the wayside was the

Malcolm Baldrige National Quality Award. Created in 1987, the award became the goal of an increasing number of organizations, its Criteria for Performance Excellence setting the standard for the cultural change that would lead to increased productivity.

At first, mainly very large corporations entered the yearly competition. Chasing it was an expensive pastime, and we're talking in some cases about millions of dollars. Companies like Motorola Inc., Xerox Corporation, Cadillac Motor Division, IBM, and Solectron were among the first winners. Within several years a small business award was added, then one for the service industries—the FedEx Corporation and the Ritz Carlton Hotel Company being among the first winners in that category. Then, the education, nonprofit, and healthcare sectors were included, awards being handed out in each of these categories when qualified applicants appeared.

But eventually, as so often happens in our society, interest began to wane. This occurred partially because not all of the winners rode happily off into the sunset. In fact, quite a few of them ran into serious problems soon after their moment of glory, problems that should have been avoided if their organization's culture had really changed, if it had truly taken on the characteristics we have been talking about.

The competition is still on, efforts are continually being made to improve the "criteria for performance excellence," but the luster is off—and for good reason. Quite simply (and here we go again): *the Baldrige Award Criteria for Performance Excellence continues to emphasize the wrong things.*

How It's Done: Or, Stars in Their Eyes

The process that occurs when an organization decides to enter the Malcolm Baldrige Award competition works something like this: The CEO or board of directors makes the decision and then announces it to the executive corps, a subgroup of which is given responsibility for planning the effort. This group decides to start by composing a comprehensive list of objectives that will help the organization meet the Baldrige standards. It usually takes the team around a year to complete this exercise.

After the list of objectives is completed, management then leads the effort to educate the workforce about what is going on. This education effort also helps generate enthusiasm for the process. Next, teams are formed around projects, usually after participants have been trained in team-building skills. This is the empowerment phase. Each team has a manager assigned to "champion" its solutions when they are presented to the upper ranks.

Eventually, lower-level employees are encouraged to submit project ideas. But every idea must be OK'd by the executives before a team is formed to address it.

Upper-level management remains deeply involved as the effort progresses, and enthusiasm remains high. The list of accomplishments grows. The amount of savings generated by individual projects also grows. And eventually, the company wins the Baldrige...

Real nice, a happy ending to our movie; we can finish our popcorn and go on home. But unfortunately, in a vast majority of cases, this is not even close. More likely, the company gives it a good try but doesn't win because each category has only one winner. In this more likely scenario, the question that immediately arises is, Should we try again next year? The improvements that have occurred as a result of the process are appreciated, but the preparations have been expensive—consultants, process-related training, team members' time away from work, the formation of a quality improvement department. Has the effort really been cost-effective? And does our company indeed have a real chance of winning? To win the Baldrige would be a tremendous public relations coup, but what are the odds of doing so, especially against competitors willing to spend more money than we can afford?

The CEO and other executives of organizations that do win the award typically travel around telling the company's story, cashing in on the spotlight. Lower-level employees also are frequently sent out to do the same. The company provides advice to newer contestants, as is required. The team effort also continues, but with less enthusiasm, and eventually, inevitably, when top-level management moves on to other priorities, the "new culture" of which the teams have been a part begins to fade.

Time to throw in another loaded statement...*As with the Crosby model, it is difficult to find Baldrige Award winners from the early days that still maintain the organization modifications responsible for their victory.* Most have reverted to the old way of getting things done, with a few of the process-related changes remaining in place. This fact engenders more questions: How far from those old ways did these companies actually stray during their drive toward the Baldrige? What real changes actually occurred?

Let's see: Communications patterns remained basically the same during this period. All the important decisions concerning team projects were still made by the bosses. The human resources department was still responsible for defining process-related training needs. Long-range objectives were still defined by the executive corps. The CEO and his or her direct reports still led the charge; they still took responsibility for drumming up enthusiasm, for leading the pep rallies.

What real changes occurred, you ask? A few new wrinkles, perhaps; employees were more involved in helping design improvements. But actually, we find very little that we could call new in terms of managing the process.

There are a lot of problems here. Many people do not understand why Deming, Ackoff, and Drucker as well as other leaders who helped shape the modern-day world of business theory have expressed misgivings concerning the efficacy of the Baldrige criteria, and why these men say, as we do, that it focuses on the wrong things and that, above all, it is not systemic.

In a March 9, 1991, letter entitled, "Comments on the 1991 Application Guidelines" (for the Baldrige), Dr. Deming remarked that although the award focuses on measurement, the most important things that organizations need to be able to measure in terms of quality improvement goals "cannot be measured." For example, he said, the effect of education and training "cannot be measured"; how well the performance of individuals and groups supports the company's objectives "cannot be measured;" the effectiveness of management in a quality improvement process, which is probably the most critical variable, "cannot be measured."

In his article "Beyond Total Quality Management," which appeared in the March 9, 1993, issue of *The Journal for Quality and Participation*, Dr. Ackoff identified other shortcomings of the Baldrige Award criteria. One is the focus on getting rid of what companies *don't want* rather than on defining and striving for what they *do want*. The purpose of measurement in the Baldrige is primarily to increase efficiencies *in existing processes*. Putting into place alternative process characteristics that we want, however, is primarily a matter of participatory planning and participatory decision making.

Another point Ackoff brought up is that the Baldrige criteria identify the customer as the major stakeholder. Information from customers helps the process define its objectives. Measuring levels of customer satisfaction eventually helps define the process' success. *But the customer is not and should not be considered the major stakeholder or the driving force behind a quality improvement effort. Customers cannot actually make the changes necessary to success. Only employees can make these changes.* Employees, therefore, must be seen as the driving force, the major stakeholder.

Another point Ackoff brought up in his article is Baldrige's lack of stress on comprehensive integration. He says that every part of the company engaged in the process goes about trying to improve its performance independently. The assumption is that if every part, taken separately, improves its performance, the performance of the organization as a whole will necessarily improve. *The focus of managing a successful quality improvement effort, however, must be, as we have said several times now, on improving the interactions between the parts, not just on improving the actions of the individual parts.*

But how do we measure interactions? How can we prove that they are effective, that they help improve the bottom line? How do we measure the relationship between two functions, the relationship between two employees, the level of communication, the level of mutual understanding? The answer is that we can't. The only way to truly measure the success of such a process is by looking at improvement in the long-term bottom line. Other approaches may be fun and may give clues, but they don't really tell the tale.

Why the Baldrige Will Never Produce the Desired Long-Term Results

The problem that Deming and Ackoff see with the approach the Baldrige criteria has triggered is that—despite its rigor, despite the enthusiasm it generates, despite the improvements it engenders—this approach possesses a fundamental flaw in that it, once again, tries to fit quality improvement efforts into the traditional management model instead of requiring that model to accept the changes necessary to improved quality and increased productivity.

The Baldrige has helped encourage at least some of the necessary modifications. It encourages the setting of standards. It encourages improvement in areas of leadership, strategic planning, customer and market focus, information and analysis, workforce development, process management, and business results. It gives recognition to those willing to make the effort. But the Baldrige Award does not force or even encourage companies to "go all the way." It allows them to stay on safe ground in terms of the management system guiding their efforts. It does not force change in this arena, which, more than any other, is critical to ongoing success.

The improvement model demonstrated by most winners of the Baldrige Award continues to be top down. Management defines the projects to be worked on. Management sets priorities. Management makes the final decisions. Management decides who is in charge of implementation. Management oversees implementation.

Although this model encourages improved performance through the reduction of errors and through the evaluation and redesign of important processes, it does not move very far toward more effective utilization of employee expertise, though this is one of the award's criteria. "Realizing the full potential of the workforce" is, in fact, listed as a human resources department objective. This leads one to believe that the involved improvement is meant to be accomplished through training rather than through empowerment.

The only approach to generating employee commitment that really works, the only one that has proved to be effective in the long run is the *full* empowerment approach we have spent so much time stressing. The critical ingredient to successful quality improvement is *not* acquiring the best possible technology. The key is *not* developing the most appropriate performance and product standards. A company can have the best technology available and still fail if the employees using that technology are not committed. A company can have the best standards in the industry and still fail if its employees don't take them seriously.

On the other hand, a company can start with inferior technology and can prevail if its employees are given ownership of that technology. This is what happened at Harley Davidson, one of the most impressive success stories of modern times. A company also can start out with lousy standards and end up with the best if employees are given the chance to help improve them.

Organizations Tend to Crumble without True Integration

A second serious flaw found in the Baldrige criteria is that, as Ackoff has said, they do not require the organization-wide integration that provides the foundation for effective change. Although the Baldrige strives to get everyone involved, integration of the efforts going on all over the organization usually occurs only at the top of the management hierarchy. Lower-level teams enjoy very little, if any, direct interaction with others who might contribute to or be affected by their projects.

For example, as has been pointed out, in efforts to win the Baldrige, the formulation of long-range objectives occurs at the beginning of the process and is accomplished by top-level managers. Only after these objectives have been decided upon is the workforce asked to get involved. Lower-level employees, the ones most responsible for achievement of these objectives, have little say in formulating them. This is not real integration.

For example, process-related training is usually designed solely by the human resources function rather than being designed with the input of team members, the people who know best what is needed. This is not real integration.

In summation, even though it is headed in the right direction, too much is still missing from the Baldrige model for it to produce the desired results. The only model for quality improvement efforts that is truly comprehensive, the only model that has proven itself, is the Systems model. This is the model that serious efforts must adopt.

Chapter 8

Who Makes the Most Productive Executive?

New CEOs frequently make an "in-your-face" entrance announcing their arrival by instituting immediate, radical changes. Several reasons can be identified for this attitude. One is the desire to impress the board members who hired them. Boards tend to begin the search for a new CEO when their bottom line is in trouble, when they're seeking new technical expertise or a cultural shift and want quick results.

A second reason for this radical behavior is the desire to impress Wall Street by showing that the company is on the move. A third reason, perhaps most important, is the desire to show that they have assumed command. One executive who had just gone through such an exercise with a new CEO compared it to a male dog marking his territory.

The new CEO huddles immediately with his or her direct reports, tells them what he or she has in mind, then gives marching orders that cascade down through the organization. Sometimes the action is well thought out, sometimes not, but rarely does it produce the desired results and quite frequently it backfires so that the company reverts quietly to the tried-and-true while pretending the innovation was a success.

This issue has again become a point of conversation due to an announcement by the new head of Yahoo!, Marissa Mayer, that employees have to come to the office every day rather than working at home, that if they don't want to do so they should start looking for a new job.

What was behind the announcement? It is well known that Yahoo!'s bottom line is currently not where stockholders want it to be. But the way the announcement was made indicated a "Just want you to know that I'm running the show now" attitude as well. Or maybe Dr. Mayer was thinking in terms of efficiencies, in terms of the quickest and least expensive way to begin making the changes she wanted to make. When one looks at her academic interests and training, this emphasis on the efficiency of action is a distinct possibility.

In the traditional workplace the most efficient approach to interaction is to follow Frederick Taylor's Scientific Management model. One person makes the decisions and then defines workforce responsibilities concerning those decisions. When a manager is making the important decisions, he or she needs information from all over the organization. Obviously, the manager wants the required input available immediately, and the most efficient way to have it available immediately is to make sure all employees come to work every day and are in their offices sitting by their phones.

One online commenter, obviously an executive or the head of a smaller company, said he agreed with Dr. Mayer's decision. He wanted his reports available at a moment's notice. He wanted to be able to call them into his office for face-to-face conversations whenever the desire struck, and if they were working at home, this obviously would not be possible.

This commenter, of course, was espousing the traditional "boss" model of upper-level management still popular in much of the corporate world. "I am ultimately responsible for our performance. Therefore, I want to have total access to what is going on and to be involved in all decisions that I want to be involved in."

Managers work hard and make serious sacrifices to rise through the ranks of a company. They don't want anything or anyone to threaten their progress or success and therefore tend to maintain tight control, to function like bosses, rather than facilitators.

Making Sure That Employees Earn Their Salary

To further emphasize this point, I can give a personal experience from my days as corporate manager of organization design with a Fortune 500 corporation headquartered in Manhattan. I was part of a five-person team that provided services to the mills our company owned. Eventually, the team members discovered that we all lived roughly in the same part of Connecticut. The decision was made that instead of spending at least an hour on the train or in a car traveling to work each day either to remain there or to head for the airport, we would design our projects and write our reports at home, gathering at somebody's house when the need arose. And when it was time to fly out we would drive directly to the airport.

Our productivity increased—until one day our team leader was called into the office of the vice president of human resources and asked why everybody had vanished. When the team leader explained our new arrangement, his boss frowned, "Sorry, Ron, but I can't allow that. I want to be able to walk past your office and see that you're earning your salary. Also, other people are beginning to ask why they can't work at home as well. If this thing spread you could get me into serious trouble."

That was approximately 25 years ago, when what we were attempting was new. In modern times it is estimated that 70 percent of US companies are allowing and even encouraging employees to work at home. Concerning research on the effectiveness of "techno-commuting," most of that which I have found touts the involved benefits and says employees are more productive when allowed to work from home. The advantages are obvious. They include the money and time not wasted commuting, the rent saved on office space, the decrease in traffic and pollution, a less disruptive environment, greater control over one's time at work, and a less exhausting lifestyle.

Of course, without someone roaming the halls to make sure nobody is slacking off there is a greater chance of people taking advantage of the situation, maybe watching television for a while or walking the dog, or changing a diaper. But then, people are still expected to complete a certain amount of work, and ways exist to gauge their productivity. Also, in many of the companies that encourage techno-commuting, one or two days are still spent in a central office or in other gathering places so that people and groups can get together with those from other departments.

And, finally, anybody who has worked in a corporate office knows that no matter what the policies are, a great deal of time is spent doing things not job related. Employees spend time chatting on the phone, surfing the Internet, gossiping at the water cooler, making sure their children got home safely from school, or whatever. It is impossible to stop such non-productive activities. Maybe they are even necessary from a mental health perspective.

So, if CEO Mayer has issued her edict that everybody must come to the office in order to ensure that employees earn their salaries, she is going to be forced to spend a lot of her time roaming the hall and looking over shoulders instead of doing what CEOs usually do. Or she will need to hire professional roamers, or maybe she will need to set up a whistle-blower reward system—all three of these tactics are serious morale killers.

Another Alternative

The thing that "boss-style" CEOs need to learn is that instead of using threats to force employees to accept desired changes, the trick is to make employees *want* these changes, to make employees *support* and *encourage* these changes of their own volition. With this in mind, the question we now need to ask is that instead of delivering an ultimatum, instead of immediately going head-to-head with the current culture, what could and should CEO Mayer have done to gain the respect of her board to shape a more productive workforce? What could and should any new CEO do?

One of the best examples of "doing it right" that I have run into during my years as a consultant and professor of management theory was highlighted by Tom Peters in his *The Leadership Alliance* film discussed initially in Chapter 1. In the early 1980s a woman named Pat Carrigan took charge of the General Motors' Powertrain components plant in Bay City, Michigan, which, due to lack of productivity, was headed for a shutdown. A large part of the workforce had already been laid off; the rest of the employees were hanging on wondering who would be next.

Dr. Carrigan was not your normal plant manager. The first female in GM history to hold such a position, her background was also unusual. Before joining GM she earned a bachelor's degree in education from Michigan State University, taught for a while, then went back to the University of Michigan to pick up the skills needed to teach students with learning disabilities. Later, Dr. Carrigan returned to the University of Michigan to earn her PhD in clinical psychology. After that she taught at the university level before joining the human resources department at GM.

So, what did this new plant manager with her unusual set of skills do upon assuming command? Did she institute immediate, major changes as a means of asserting her authority, as a means of proving to all who were listening that she had personally studied the involved problems and knew how to make the company more profitable?

No, she did not. In fact, she called for no changes at all in products, manufacturing processes, or management policy.

Instead, the first thing this new plant manager did was to take the time necessary to walk around and introduce herself to as many of its approximately 2,000 employees as she could reach, shaking their hands, asking about their jobs, asking about what had been going on in the plant, about whether or not they thought the workforce could turn the situation around.

This approach is extremely different from that apparently being taken by Dr. Mayer, but the most radical part was yet to come. Shortly after making the rounds, Dr. Carrigan, instead of announcing how things were going to be done from now on, began asking workers for *their* ideas, for ways *they* thought the operation could be improved, for ways to cut costs and increase output. She encouraged but did not force the workers in different parts of the operation to form teams. The role of these teams was not only to come up with improvements but to take charge of implementing and monitoring the improvements once they were agreed to by other functions that would be affected.

Personality or Training?

The differences between the Pat Carrigan "facilitator" model and the "boss" model Marissa Mayer chose at least initially to institute upon assuming her new post are stark. One has to wonder if they are the result of conditioning/education or of genetics? Concerning education, Dr. Carrigan's education was people oriented—how to teach people, how to read their actions and emotions, how to get them to do what she wanted them to do. Dr. Mayer's education was at the opposite end of the spectrum. It was based mainly on the manipulation of numerical data. Marissa earned her bachelor's degree in symbolic logic at Stanford, then her master's in computer science specializing in artificial intelligence—in the study of how to generate intelligence in machines and robots. Finally, she earned her doctorate in another quantitative field, in the field of "search."

Eventually, Dr. Mayer took a job as an engineer at Google, progressing from that position into the ranks of management. Dr. Mayer has made important contributions in the realm of high tech and will probably make more. But while Pat Carrigan's skills have proven foundational to her success as a manager, will those of Marissa Mayer do the same?

And what about the genetic question? Was Dr. Carrigan born to be a people-oriented person, did her genetic composition aim her toward teaching? And did Dr. Mayer's genes guide her toward the challenge of more logical problems that can be quantified, that are not obfuscated by nonquantifiable factors such as emotions and needs and morale?

The obvious answer to our initial question, long known, is that both conditioning/education and genes help shape an individual's personality and abilities. It's the old left-brain, right-brain argument. According to the theory of left-brain or right-brain dominance, each side of the brain controls a different type of thinking. Left-brained oriented people are considered to be better at such things as logic, language, critical thinking, and numbers. Right-brain oriented people are considered to be better at dealing with people, at reading and expressing emotions, at thinking intuitively, and at tasks calling for creativity.

From Bully to Technology Expert

So, which type of thinking is best for managers to depend on? History tells us that during the early years of the Industrial Revolution when companies began to grow in size from usually fewer than 50 workers to a hundred or several hundred, neither type of thinking was relevant. The first-line supervisor's main responsibility was to use whatever means necessary to keep workers at their task, to make sure that they "earned their salaries," which, at that point, were their only incentive. Those in upper-level management, those making the decisions, rarely spoke to or heard from lower-level employees. The decision-making process was strictly top down with little or no input from anyone below. The only thing flowing upward was production data.

As technology grew more complex, however, requirements in terms of managerial skills changed. At that point, the employee who best understood the involved technology was selected for the managerial role. Emphasis was on making sure that process flow was uninterrupted. If a machine broke down, the need was to have somebody on the spot who could take charge of repairs immediately and make sure they were completed in the shortest possible amount of time.

This was the period during which dominant left-brain thinking came into vogue. Increasing the productivity of machines, not of employees, was the objective. Employees functioned mainly as extensions of machines, and machines have no emotions, making right-brain abilities unimportant. All that machines needed to remain productive during this era was a steady stream of electricity. All that employees needed to remain productive was their salaries. To the left-brain executives in charge—those who believed that if a variable couldn't be quantified, it wasn't important to the success of the organization—this made good sense; this was logical.

From Technology Expert to People Expert

As we moved into the modern era, however, three things occurred that forced change, things that greatly influenced the role of management. First, technology rapidly became too complex for any one person to have all the answers. As a result of this evolution, technological issues in organizations of any size were turned over to a department staffed by experts, though not even the focused attention of these experts was, in a growing number of instances, sufficient. Anybody who has dealt with a corporate information technology (IT) department knows that its members are continuously struggling with increasingly complex and frequently unexpected challenges.

Second, modern-day employees are generally better educated and better trained than their predecessors so that they are increasingly capable of solving at least low-level technology problems themselves. As a combined result of the creation of IT departments and the increased level of training received by employees, therefore, bosses are no longer turned to when such problems arise so that the need for left-brain dominance as a prerequisite for success as a manager has diminished.

Third, salary no longer suffices as an incentive. Due partially to their rising level of education, employees are expecting more to offset the increasing amount of job-related responsibility being shouldered. Among the things being asked for are more respect from management, more challenging work, more opportunity for advancement, increased education benefits, more control over their time, more say in the production process, and profit sharing. Just getting rid of employees when their level of productivity falls short doesn't work anymore except at the lowest tiers of the service industry, at the Walmarts and McDonald's, where minimal knowledge of technology and processes is required, necessitating minimal levels of training and minimal incentives. As this knowledge requirement increases, however, and the involved expense reaches a certain range, it becomes more cost-effective to improve salaries and other incentives than to let them go.

Management's challenge has changed. The focus has shifted from expertise in technology to expertise in dealing with individual employees and with employee systems. The important question now is, How do I get the most productivity out of the employees I manage? The type of thinking required for successfully answering that question has moved from left brain to right brain. The employees themselves have taken on the traditional left-brain responsibilities. The manager's role is now to understand both emotionally and intellectually his or her reports, to facilitate their learning, and to develop a reward system that encourages them. All these are largely right-brain activities.

Can Left-Brain Thinkers Demonstrate Right-Brain Talents?

As a result of this shift, one must assume that the Marissa Mayerses of the world are at a disadvantage in managerial roles. As project team leaders in high-tech industries, they are probably without equal, their talent matched to the challenge. But in terms of maximizing the productivity of a workforce, the Pat Carrigans seem to enjoy an advantage in the modern-day workplace.

The next question, therefore, has to be: Is it possible for a left-brain thinker to acquire and exhibit the skills of a right-brain thinker? Genetic patterns are pretty well set. But if the appropriate incentive is offered can they be changed? Human beings have been defined by scientists as "purposeful" systems. This means that they are capable not only of defining their individual purpose along with the best way to achieve it but also of changing both their definition of purpose and their definition of the best way to achieve it. Based on this logic, the answer to our question should be yes.

For a person to change successfully, however, several things are required. The first is the realization that a more effective alternative exists. The second is an understanding of what is needed to precipitate the desired change. And this is the point at which conditioning/education comes into play. Where do we get that conditioning/education? Some of it is absorbed from an organization's culture. Some of it comes from corporate-sponsored training sessions. But most of it, at this point in time at least, comes from the education system.

When we look at the typical undergraduate college business department curriculum, we see mainly left-brain challenges—finance, accounting, economics, business law, strategy and policy, information systems, human resources management, supply chain management. The only traditional requirement that might incorporate right-brain thinking is organization behavior. The involved curriculum in this course might include, for example, the classification of worker attitudes as well as lessons on how to shape or influence these attitudes. Most current organization behavior texts also include a section on team building—the best way to put teams together, to run teams, and to make them productive.

But this is just one course out of 20-some in the major, so that business department program emphasis is still on left-brain thinking. No courses, for example, directly address the psychology of the individual, how to motivate the individual.

Where the Real Problem Lies

At the undergraduate level this overemphasis on left-brain thinking might be understandable. Undergraduate students need to gain familiarity with all the functions of an organization. A majority of students will not move immediately into workplace management positions. As a result, they need initially to develop a left-brain skill set or left-brain skill sets that will help them find employment.

The problem becomes more serious, however, when after several years in the workplace, employees are ready to move into management positions, when they return to the university for their MBA. This graduate-level degree was developed to give employees the expertise necessary to function as effective managers. Unfortunately, concerning MBA curriculum, one finds the same left-brain emphasis found in undergraduate programs. Typically, courses in this curriculum cover finance, accounting, economics, information technology, operations management, strategy, and policy. Again, frequently, only one course, perhaps Organizational Leadership, has to do with right-brain thinking and concerns working directly with employees.

Obviously, a need exists to enrich at least MBA programs. They need to encourage more of a right-brain perspective. Pat Carrigan was a trained psychologist and therapist. She freely admitted her lack of expertise concerning the parts manufactured at the Bay City plant as well as the involved manufacturing processes. She did not believe, however, that she needed such expertise. Her job, as she understood it, was to find ways to make her employees more productive.

Dr. Carrigan's management philosophy was built around an understanding that people generally do what they are rewarded for doing, so she spent her time looking for ways to reward the employees working with her, be it by shaking their hand and smiling, by asking for their ideas, by giving them the power to design and implement their suggestions, by making sure they knew what was going on throughout the organization. All these activities are right brain or have a strong right-brain component.

Pat Carrigan, during her time at the Bay City plant, provided a good example of the facilitator model for management, a model that requires right-brain thinking. MBA programs should shift their curriculum in that direction. Their major objective should be to provide the mind-set and skills required for managers to be good *facilitators* rather than simply *bosses*.

Chapter 9

How to Design More Profitable Businesses

The concept that needs to be introduced once more at this stage of the conversation and seriously explored is *system thinking*, a concept very much in vogue 25 years ago that eventually fell out of favor, overshadowed by more quantitative schools of thought. The Systems approach is built on two pillars: The first, as has been said, is the belief that "the whole is more than the sum of its parts." This means, basically, that the interactions between the parts of any system—be it a car, a person, or an organization—are just as important as the parts themselves in terms of the system meeting its objectives.

"The whole is more than the sum of its parts" in the business world has to do with organizational design, with the organization's pieces and the processes that bind them together. As stated above, "interactions between the parts" includes the interactions between individual employees, between employee teams, between departments, between divisions, and all the way up through the organization.

The second pillar of the Systems approach, not mentioned before, is the *development ethic*. It says that employees should be encouraged to develop and utilize their positive potential to the fullest possible extent to improve the quality of their work life, the quality of their life in general, and the fortunes of the company. The inputs required to do this are a reasonable salary, access to required and desired learning, a managerial system that treats them fairly and encourages development, a work environment that does not hamper their efforts, and enough time to take advantage of the other inputs.

Organizations that have become "systemic" in nature possess *four key characteristics* also mentioned before (obviously, the author wants you to remember them): First, such organizations are *truly participative* in the sense that every employee affected by a decision is allowed some level of input into that decision. Second, organization activities are *integrated on all levels and between all levels.* Third, the organization is *capable of dealing with continual change* in both the external and internal environments, change that is arriving with increasing rapidity. Fourth, organizational activities *facilitate the ongoing learning of all employees.*

So, how do we design an organization that has these characteristics, shaping the involved organization processes in such a way that they support greater productivity? Because our main objective is to make organizations more profitable, let's start by insisting that all units, support as well as production, contribute directly to the bottom line so that their progress can be measured.

Turning Support Functions into Profit Centers

Start-ups and smaller operations usually do not yet need to include comprehensive support functions such as training, recruiting, and research and development (R&D). Training occurs mainly on the job. Staff members are encouraged to share their expertise with newcomers. Old-timers want to make sure that new hires became as productive as possible as rapidly as possible in order to share the workload. Recruiting is relatively informal, with current employees frequently recommending a friend. R&D is also unsophisticated, as process improvement ideas are generated by individual employees and by teams being broadcast immediately so that feedback can be gained quickly from the rest of the staff.

Start-ups and smaller companies do not yet have to worry about organizing and paying for support activities that have no direct effect on the bottom line. But what about larger, more mature organizations that do require support functions, companies where ongoing training, no matter how it might be organized, is critical to the company's success; where steady turnover makes continual recruitment, again no matter how it might be organized, a requirement; where R&D efforts must remain continually productive for the company to stay competitive? Is it possible for a larger organization to turn these functions into profit centers as well so that they contribute directly to the bottom line?

Yes, it is.

Professor Jamshid Gharajedaghi, while a member of the Social Systems Sciences doctoral program faculty at the Wharton School, University of Pennsylvania, developed a model he called the Multilevel, Multidimensional, Modular Organization. His model incorporated six dimensions:

1. Output Units: These autonomous units are responsible for manufacturing and distributing the goods or services generated by the company.
2. Input Units: These units sell their production-related services to Output Units—services the Output Units are incapable of generating themselves such as training, recruitment, and R&D.
3. Environmental Unit: This unit helps the organization define its relationship with the external environment in terms of markets, advocacy, employee education, and community development projects. It helps facilitate and

coordinate research in these areas, selling skills and information to both Output and Input Units.

4. Planning/Decision-Making Unit: Representatives from all organization units sit on the Planning/Decision-Making Unit board. They define the organization's mission and objectives. They regulate and coordinate the activities of all organization units. They deal with decision making at the highest level.

5. Control Unit: Personnel in this unit are responsible for monitoring the organization's efforts to achieve its mission and objectives as defined by the Planning/Decision-Making Unit.

6. Management Unit: The managing director and his or her staff are responsible for facilitating the activities of the Planning/Decision-Making Unit.

To more easily meet the challenge being discussed, Gharajedaghi's Multilevel, Multidimensional, Modular Organization model can be simplified. A modified version would include the following:

■ Output Units: These are responsible for manufacturing, *marketing*, and distributing the item or service produced, thus becoming responsible for all the steps that contribute to their bottom line.

■ Input Units: These remain the same. They continue to sell services to the Output Units.

■ Management Unit: This unit is responsible for organizing and monitoring the company's ongoing strategic planning effort and for organizing, integrating, and supporting unit efforts to continually improve products, manufacturing/service delivery processes, management systems, and the work environment. The Management Unit, therefore, takes responsibility for facilitating the planning and decision-making process. It also takes over the Control

Unit function, control occurring automatically if the right model for long-range planning and decision making has been adopted along with the right reward system.

But how does the relationship between Output and Input Units in our new model differ from that found in the traditional model? In the traditional model the corporation pays the employees of Input Units salaries to deliver predefined services to Output Units. Employees of the Input Units are given no say about what these services should be, whether they should be paid for or not, and what they should cost if paid for. The only cost taken into consideration by the company is that of salaries. If, at some point, executives think money can be saved, an Input Unit is dissolved and the involved service outsourced. If the outside supplier begins raising its price, the company looks for a new supplier. If things get too bad, the company might consider reestablishing the Input Unit, which is an expensive undertaking.

But what if Input Units were converted from cost centers to profit centers as has been suggested? What if they were allowed to *sell* their service to Output Units and to set the price? A bad idea, right? Because without competition they would be free to overcharge. But what if there was, indeed, competition? What if, as Gharajedaghi suggests, Output Units were free to buy the involved service from an outside supplier if that supplier could deliver an equal quality of service more cheaply? Input Units would then be forced to come up with a quality product that was reasonably priced and to continue improving it in order to keep the business. They would become part of the free market system, living or dying by their bottom line; they would be forced to deal with real competition in the marketplace the same way that output units do.

Also, under this arrangement, because they were now profit centers, Input Units could begin looking for new customers just as Output Units do. They would be allowed to sell their services to other companies so long as no conflict of interest existed. As a result, not only would they have a bottom line of their own, but they would, at the same time, be contributing fresh income to the parent company's bottom line.

Both Output and Input Units would be able to develop new projects. An Output Unit, for example, could develop a project to sell items online. An Input Training Unit could develop and sell a training module to potential suppliers that would help them improve or shape the goods or services to be delivered. An Input Unit could also develop a model for treating employees with addiction problems and sell these services to smaller companies unable to provide them internally. New projects, according to Gharajedaghi, could be financed through loans from other units, these loans being paid back with interest. They could also be financed through the sale of shares of project stock to other units.

This model should please free-enterprise supporters. It can possibly, however, add a serious organizational problem, that of in-house competition. So, how do we address this problem? One way is by improving communication between the involved units, by more fully integrating their efforts. A second way is by reshaping reward systems so that they encourage cooperation rather than competition.

The Three-Tiered Reward System Finds a Home

The Three-Tiered Reward System, the origin of which was discussed in Chapter 5, fits well with this model. All Output and Input Unit employees will receive a salary that will constitute the smallest part of their reward during good times and will allow employees and families to survive during bad times. All Output and Input Unit employees will also receive a bonus based on their unit's profits. Finally, all employees will receive a company-wide bonus, one normally comprising the largest part of their reward in order to keep employees from focusing on the productivity of their individual units rather than on the productivity of the organization as a whole, in order to encourage organization-wide cooperation and integration.

In terms of paying Management Unit members, salaries will be supported by a tax levied on the Input and Output Units, with a percentage taken from each unit's profits. Members of the Management Unit will receive salaries like everybody else, but these salaries will be higher than the ones received by the rest of the workforce because while Output and Input Unit managers will be eligible for a share of their unit-level bonus, executive-level managers who are part of the Management Unit will not. Management Unit members, however, will be eligible to share in the company-wide bonus. This bonus will be divided equally among all employees, thus further encouraging cooperation. The company-wide bonus will be drawn from the tax revenues paid by Output and Input Units after Management Unit member salaries have been taken out.

The Circular Organization Management Systems Design

Obviously, a lot of decisions need to be made when an organization adopts the modified Multilevel, Multidimensional, Modular Organization model and the Three-Tiered Reward System. These decisions include what support services should be offered in-house, what unit projects should the company invest in if no other units want to loan the money or purchase stock in the project, how much executives should be paid, the amount of the yearly company-wide bonus which in turn determines the amount of unit bonuses. The body making these decisions will be a hierarchy of boards responsible for managerial decisions. These boards lie at the core of the Circular Organization concept that was introduced by Professor Russell Ackoff, architect of the University of Pennsylvania

Social Systems Sciences doctoral program and later head of ACASA (the Ackoff Center for Advanced Systems Approaches).

In an organization of any size, a hierarchy of managers is required so that decision-making responsibility can be delegated effectively and the decision-making process itself can be facilitated and integrated. Policies governing this process can vary greatly. In companies that have decided on the Circular Organization approach, each manager, starting at lowest level of the individual Output Unit and Input Unit hierarchy, has a "board of directors" on which he or she sits. Other members of each board are the manager's direct reports, be they low-level workers or other managers, and the boss of the manager whose board it is. The direct reports, if they are also managers, of course have their own boards and bring along input from *their* direct reports, who also have boards. As a result, any manager above the lowest level receives input, direct or indirect, from three levels below and three levels above. Boards can also invite representatives from other units who might make a contribution to take part in meetings. Obviously, this approach encourages the integration of efforts.

Each board's responsibilities include the following:

1. Planning for the unit whose board it is. The plans, of course, must fit with those of the board representing the level above, creating an upward cascading effect, all plans eventually fitting with and supporting the plan generated by the highest-level board, that of the CEO. Boards are also responsible for constantly modifying their unit's plan, taking into account a changing environment while making sure the involved modifications continue to support planning objectives of the level above, which are also constantly being modified.

2. Policy making for the unit whose board it is. Policies are rules of the game, how things should be done. For example, a higher-level policy might be that the company promotes current employees into vacant executive positions

whenever possible as opposed to looking for somebody from outside the organization. A lower-level policy might be that employees can modify their working hours within certain limits.

3. Coordinating the plans and policies of the immediate lower level. This effort is facilitated by the fact that the managers of the involved lower-level units all sit on the board doing the coordinating.

4. Integrating the board's plans and policies with those of lower-level and higher-level units. This effort is again facilitated by the fact that the managers of the involved units all sit on the board doing the integrating.

5. Improving the quality of work life of those at the level the board governs, providing a process by which all reports can identify possible improvements in products generated or services offered, in manufacturing processes or in service delivery processes, in management systems, in the work environment. The board will then encourage employees on all levels to design these improvements and to implement them. The individual boards can spin off modified task forces that work on unit improvement projects. The term *modified task force* is used because the traditional task force is formed to come up with a suggested improvement and a suggested design, but is then disbanded and has nothing to do with implementation. Members of the modified task force suggest an improvement and, after the board or boards involved approve it, also take responsibility for designing and implementing that improvement. A level board can also agree with the level board of another unit or of other units to create a modified task force including employees from both units to work together on a project that crosses unit lines.

6. Evaluate on an ongoing basis the performance of the manager whose board it is. Boards cannot fire their leader but can make recommendations to upper-level

management. Also, a new manager selected by upper-
level management to fill the board's leadership position
cannot be hired without the approval of board members.

What these level boards do, of course, is take over the
major responsibilities of management. The manager whose
board it is becomes mainly a facilitator, making sure that the
board's efforts remain focused on the organization's long-term
objectives, facilitating and helping integrate the efforts of his
or her board with those of other boards.

Modified Task Force Rules

All modified task forces involved in designing and implementing organization improvements must abide by a set of preestab-
lished rules similar to the ground rules laid out for a systemic
quality improvement effort. These rules includes the following:

1. Members must meet formally once a week for one hour;
   the involved employees are released from their regular
   responsibility for this period of time. One of the major
   reasons for failure of such efforts is that team members or
   their bosses decide they are too busy to attend meetings.
   If one member misses, others are more likely to begin
   missing as well.
2. Modified task force meetings must be held during working hours. Forcing workers to add time to their workday,
   even if they are paid for that time, is a display of disre-
   spect and will have a negative effect on commitment.
3. Modified task force members have access to all company
   personnel who might contribute information important to
   the project. Either the source will be invited to a meeting
   or a member of the modified task force will contact that
   person. Those contacted for input will have one week
   to reply. The response might be, "Here is the desired

information," or, "Yes, I'll attend your next meeting," or, "No, but I will deliver the desired information as soon as possible," with a date set.

4. Projects that might affect the performance of other units in the organization must be agreed to by those units. The units must be asked for input and must agree to the model developed before the originating unit can begin implementing it.

5. Projects cannot be taken over by outside managers who become interested. This is another surefire way to destroy the value of a modified task force. A managerial take-over destroys the sense of process ownership necessary to developing employee commitment to both the project and the process. While a project takeover might produce quicker short-term results, its cost to the organization as a whole will be much greater in the long run.

6. Any improvement suggested by a modified task force must be justified by a cost-benefit analysis when possible or by a quality-of-working-life rationale when not possible. This requirement is important for several reasons. First, it requires group members to discover whether the proposed change is economically viable or not. Second, it forces group members to think improvements through thoroughly. Third, it is a major part of the ongoing education process, as group members learn what the unit's priorities are and, when the unit cannot afford to finance the involved improvement itself, what the company's priorities are and how this project fits in with other projects being submitted by modified task forces formed by other level boards in other functions.

The Circular Organization approach is obviously systemic. In terms of participation, all managers are directly involved. Workers gain a say through elected representatives on the lowest-level board. In terms of integration, every manager sits on several boards on several levels. Concerning the ability to deal with continual change in the environment, because input is continual and from all over the organization, companies using the Circular Organization approach are more capable of doing so. And finally, concerning ongoing learning, everyone involved has access to the information flowing horizontally and vertically through the board network; everyone is expected to make effective use of that information when helping to formulate decisions.

The question of time, of course, comes up. "If I as a manager sit on several boards—mine, my boss's, and those of my direct reports—when do I have time to get my work done?" The answer is that, in actuality, the boards are meeting most of your managerial challenges. Your main responsibility is no longer to make all the decisions yourself, but to facilitate the efforts of your board's members to contribute.

Planning from a Systems Perspective

We now have defined a way to make every function in an organization as profitable as possible, to allow all Output and Input Units to contribute directly to the bottom line. Also, we have come up with a reward system approach that encourages every employee to be as productive as possible. Finally, we have offered a management system design that ensures the most effective use of employee expertise and integrates efforts thoroughly throughout the organization.

The main thing missing at this point is a way to best define the organization's role in society, what it should offer, what markets it should compete in, and how it should compete. Decisions in this realm are made during a planning exercise that defines both long-term objectives and short-term goals. For the best results during this exercise, one needs to apply the same requirements applied to the other systems designs presented. The planning effort must be participative, integrated organization-wide, capable of dealing with continual change, and it must encourage ongoing learning.

Most current strategic planning models lack these characteristics. They are either top down or bottom up. Companies that practice top-down planning usually have a department or hire a consulting firm that spends its time using a wide range of tools and techniques to identify environmental trends—trends in the marketplace, trends in terms of requisite supplies, societal trends—and making recommendations built around these trends. Based on the recommendations, top management defines its objectives for the next year or two, then passes them on down through the levels so that departments know what is expected of them.

The major problem with this approach is the lack of input from lower levels during the definition of objectives and goals. Top management's focus is different from that of lower-level employees. Top-level management might have a more global perspective and know what direction it wants the firm to go, but frequently it lacks an understanding of how things are currently working down below—the organization's current strengths and weaknesses—an understanding that is necessary to successful implementation of its plan.

Organizations that practice bottom-up planning send out word that each lower-level unit needs to come up with a plan, usually one including a wish list of items or updates needed. These plans are then sent up to the next level, where they are consolidated, that level incorporating them into its own plan. This progression continues until the highest level is reached, where top management decides who gets what and passes the word back down.

The major problem with this approach is that units have little or no idea of how the changes they wish to make fit into the whole. Sometimes these changes will conflict with changes being asked for by other units. Frequently there is not enough money available to fund all requests. Due to the lack of communication and of integration, employees, when they are turned down, often do not understand why.

The type of planning being suggested for companies that desire to become more productive and profitable is *interactive planning*, which is all-over-at-once and possesses the systemic characteristics required for improving the bottom line. Every planning paradigm includes four major phases. The first involves defining the current situation, internal and external, identifying the organization's strengths and weaknesses, opportunities and threats found in the external environment with a focus on the market environment. A majority of planning paradigms begin with this phase then move on to the second phase, creating a list of improvements the company wishes to make and then prioritizing that list. The third phase involves deciding what resources are available and which projects they should be allocated to before outlining the steps that should be taken in each project. The fourth phase is watching the implementation process as it unfolds to ensure that it stays on track and to make changes when necessary.

The major way in which interactive planning differs from traditional planning is that after defining the current situation, instead of starting where the organization is, identifying needed improvement and prioritizing them, interactive planning uses a technique called *idealized design* to help the organization identify how it would like to function ideally, what it ought to produce and sell ideally. Every part of the organization is presented with the same challenge: "When you came in this morning, the organization was gone, completely gone, nothing was left. Your job is to redesign your part of it. It is to decide what products/services should be offered ideally, to decide how they should be designed, to decide how they should be manufactured or delivered, to decide what technology is needed, to decide how best the operation should be managed, to decide how the work environment should be shaped to achieve maximum productivity and profitability."

Only after the idealized designs from all levels have been generated and integrated does implementation begin. But instead of making just piecemeal improvements, the process now has a target to aim for. The question in terms of prioritization now becomes, Which improvements get us closest to the target (the ideal) the fastest?

Idealized design is obviously participative; every employee can be involved in the design of his or her part of the operation if he or she wants. It is obviously integrated organization-wide; all the design must work together before priorities are set and implementation begins. The model developed can obviously deal with continual change because it is flexible and ongoing, information constantly being fed into it by the hierarchy of boards that are responsible for facilitation. And finally, continual learning is obviously occurring all over the organization because all employees on all levels are involved.

So, that's it, that's a way to make organizations more profitable by turning Input Units into profit centers alongside Output Units, and by instituting a reward system that strongly encourages cooperation among employees, that creates a management system designed to make maximum use of everybody's expertise, and that includes a planning paradigm that features an effective vehicle for developing the necessary overview and for setting priorities.

Every part of the model proposed in this chapter is a radical departure from what we are used to. Substantial changes in the way companies are organized and run would be required if it these parts were to be implemented. Therefore, what is being offered will most likely be seen as a threat in most management circles. But at least the model gives us an ideal to focus on, a target to aim for as we feel our way along in the realm of organization development.

Chapter 10

The Matter of Ethics

Which comes first in organizations, ethical behavior or the generation of a culture that has the characteristics we've been stressing all through this book—a truly participative management system, the integration of all activities, the ability to deal effectively with ongoing change in both the internal and external environments, the encouragement of continual learning for all employees?

Must an ethical climate be in place for these characteristics to be generated? Or does this set of characteristics, more than any others, encourage ethical behavior; does such a climate make ethical behavior attractive to those who might be tempted to stray? Does it make getting away with unethical behavior more difficult?

It is, of course, possible to find ethical behavior in organizations where the management philosophy does not necessarily encourage these characteristics. Many such organizations exist. Most are led by an extremely powerful, visible father figure or by CEOs who provide an example and encourage everyone to follow suit.

On the other hand, a growing number of business leaders believe that rather than placing major emphasis on setting the example and fortifying individual employees against temptation, emphasis should be place on defining the man-agement philosophy and on designing the organization's key processes in ways that keep temptation from arising. Unethical behavior is found less frequently in such organizations because it is less rewarding. The situations that encourage it do not arise as frequently because they have been designed out of existence.

Sounds Good, But…

The problem is that the number of such companies, though growing, remains relatively small. Most organizations have been unwilling to make the leap, despite growing evidence of its value. They like what they hear about the resultant increased profits and improved morale. They make a point of reading up on it. But when the time comes to put the approach into place, to actually make the necessary changes, they hesitate, then stick with the tried and true, with the present classroom case studies (What would you do in this situation? What *should* you do in this situation?), and then afterward reprogram the individual employee approach. So maybe once, twice, or four times a year staff are summoned to a seminar to receive a lecture, then to join a discussion group assigned a case study to review, after which they take part in a role-playing exercise. Following this supposedly transforma-tional experience, everybody returns to his or her job, where nothing has changed—the same pressures and temptations exist, they are expected to put into practice what they have learned while receiving no reward for doing so other than personal gratification, and trying to implement the necessary changes might actually get them branded as a troublemaker.

Or, if companies do decide to try the process redesign approach, they go at it piecemeal, paying attention only to the parts they feel comfortable with. Then, when the desired improvement in ethics does not occur, they say that the model doesn't work or that it takes too long to produce results, so they drop it and move on to the next quick fix.

I recently asked a group of 15 middle-level managers from 15 different organizations why their company's efforts to improve ethics and to modernize were not producing the desired results. Their answers included the following:

1. Lack of visible commitment; lack of a believable message from top management
2. No real effort to get buy-in from employees, mainly lip-service and pep rallies
3. Not sticking to one approach, piling one approach on top of another
4. Emphasis on short-term rather than long-term results
5. Using the threat of punishment as a prime motivator
6. Rather than focusing on the challenge, focusing on dealing with intimidation from bosses
7. Difficulty of changing old habits
8. Leadership turnover with constantly changing rules of the game
9. Corporate aversion to risk-taking of any sort
10. Unwillingness to argue with the success (no matter how meager) previously enjoyed by doing things the old way
11. The inability or unwillingness to learn from the success of other companies

Sound familiar? All of the above are valid criticisms of organizational attempts to improve ethics. But they are all also just symptoms. They are not the cause of failure. The cause lies much deeper, in the culture of the organization, in the culture spawned by the traditional management system. Also, the "cause" is not singular. It is a collection of intertwined, inseparable factors that we can call "producers," factors that reinforce each other.

And the Really Hard Part Is…

To truly improve the ethical climate of an organization, we need to change the entire organization—its culture, its mind-set, the way employees on all levels are influenced by key processes. But instead of first developing an understanding of the whole, of the entire network of problems that must be addressed, companies that do decide to try the redesign approach usually dive precipitously into change. The result of this impatience is that they end up focusing on individual parts and individual processes, as they had previously focused on individual employees, which doesn't cut it. They paint the room a lighter shade of blue to make it appear bigger rather than actually knocking a wall out.

Meanwhile, frustration levels begin to rise as market conditions demand more attention to the numbers at the expense of the human side of the equation. Those heading the change effort say that empowerment leads to improved ethics, that the organization needs to give employees more access to information, and that the company needs to involve employees more in decisions; and at the same time, the managers, who are running the nuts and bolts and are driven by market forces and by concern about keeping their jobs, tighten controls, take more authority onto themselves so that mistakes are less likely to occur, and depend increasingly on the threat of punishment to discourage unethical behavior.

The stories of Bernard Madoff, Kenneth Lay, Jeffrey Skilling, Bernie Ebbers, Scott Rothstein, Dennis Kozlowski, Richard Scrushy, Sam Waksal, Joseph Forte, and others as poster children for the dark side of the ethics debate are only the latest in a long history of publicly admired, then reviled corporate leaders. A while back, it was Albert J. Dunlap, better known as "Chainsaw Al," who laid off about 20 percent of the workforce at Crown Zellerbach while CEO there, one-third of the workforce at Scott Paper, and more than 6,000 at Sunbeam before being fired—not because of his tactics, but because those tactics didn't produce the bottom-line results he had promised. Dunlap and those who admired him so fiercely obviously number among the hot dogs we talked about in Chapter 3, driven more so by their competitive instincts (adolescent arrest?) and their egos than by common sense, and certainly not by the respect for employees that history has proven to be the more effective incentive.

Ethical problems in most organizations, however, cannot usually be traced to individual managers or to their personal failings. Rather, the producers of the involved problems lies with the management philosophy they are weaned on, such as the graduate management programs (MBAs) that continuing to focus on the numbers while giving only lip service the other side of the coin, and with the management systems they have designed or fallen heir to. It is these management systems, rather than a lack of character on the part of those involved, that spawn the decisions that encourage and sometimes force employees to act unethically. Too frequently, managers either do not understand the ethical implications of their design decisions, or they do understand the implications and the effect these decisions will have on the activities of employees but cannot come up with a better alternative.

Employees Would Be a Lot Easier to Deal with if They Weren't So Damn Human

A tug-of-war arises around the issue of which values should shape the ethical climate of the organization. On the one hand, some think solely in growth-driven terms where *growth* is defined only with numbers that are *value-free* in terms of ethics. Employees represent a major chunk of these numbers, so the employees are treated as though they are value-free as well, which means that they have no values of their own, that their only values are those assigned by the company.

On the other hand, some organizations are moving toward an ethic that continues to focus on the numbers but incorporate them into a larger context that includes nonquantifiable factors as well, factors such as morale, ethics, and cooperation. In this context employees are allowed to become *value-full*—allowed to have personal values of their own that need to be taken into consideration when management decisions are made.

Probably the most prominent characteristic shared by leaders of the latter type of organization is their inherent or learned respect for employees, for employees' values and needs, and for employee potential, and their belief in management's responsibility for facilitating the realization of that potential. Ralph Stayer, CEO of the highly successful Johnsonville Sausage, whom we mentioned previously, with his belief that it is immoral for business leaders not to allow and encourage employees to develop their talents as fully as possible, is a good modern-day example of this attitude and its benefits.

Stayer has a well-known historic precedent to support his actions. In the early 1900s Henry Ford stunned the world by doubling the wage of employees at his motor company while shortening the workday. He also provided education, counseling, and a company store with relatively cheap prices. He believed the major purpose of business to be the betterment of society. He decided that if all his employees could earn enough to buy a car of their own, Ford as well as the overall economy would benefit.

Ford, in turn, had a historic precedent to model *himself* on. During the early 1800s Robert Owen partly owned and ran one of the largest textile mills in Scotland. Going against the current "economic man" management philosophy (the only purpose in life should be to make money, no matter what the cost to others), he treated his workforce and their families with respect, paid them relatively well, cut the number of hours spent in the mill, educated young employees, and provided relatively good housing and a well-run community.

As with Ford, his attitude made him extremely successful and extremely wealthy.

All three of these men demonstrated or, in the case of Stayer, are demonstrating a high degree of respect for their employees, Ford and Owen during an era when emphasis was on getting the most productivity out of workers for the smallest amount of pay possible. All three of these men benefited greatly or are benefiting from acting ethically and from encouraging an ethical climate.

So, How Do We Figure This Thing Out?

At this point, it is necessary to ask: are the Henry Fords, the Ralph Stayers and the people who run Google more ethical than the Bernard Madoffs, the Kenneth Lays, and "Chainsaw" Al Dunlaps? Instinctively, we want to say yes. But why do we want to say yes? What is our standard for comparison?

Humans need a standard by which to measure their response when making ethical judgments. Sometimes the standard is personal, but usually it is one developed by society and tested by time. We need a standard that has been accepted universally, or at least is acceptable to most of us when making a decision with an ethical component.

That is, or course, what ethics is about, the definition of a standard by which to judge behavior. Plenty of such standards exist. Four major schools of ethical thought have evolved producing two sets of diametrically opposed approaches to deciding what is ethical and what is not. The first set pits utilitarianism against egoism. *Utilitarianism* says that the most ethical decision is that which provides the greatest good for the greatest number. Democracy is obviously a utilitarian form of governance. *Egoism*, at the other extreme, says that the most ethical decision is that which best satisfies individual needs and desires with no concern for its effect on others.

The second set of opposing schools includes deontology and relativism. *Deontologists* say that society must established a set of universal rights, the US Constitution being one example of such a set of rights, and that every citizen must be allowed to enjoy these same rights. *Relativists* say that ethical decisions must be made situation by situation, that if situational variables change, the decision might also change.

But how do we define the most appropriate approach for our workplace situation? What do we base our decision on? Are there irrefutable generic laws that clearly delineate the difference between what is right and what is wrong? Or does what is right and what is wrong vary according to the situation? Which comes first in terms of ethical decisions: the individual's belief system, that of the company, or that of society as a whole? And probably the most important question, How should the workplace perspective we have been encouraging in previous chapters influence our attempts to identify the most appropriate code of ethical behavior, the most appropriate ethical standard upon which to base workplace decisions? Lots and lots of questions, all difficult to answer.

During the last decade excesses have occurred in the US banking and stock brokerage sectors, private industry, and the nonprofit sector that have hurt employees and investors badly, that have pushed our economy almost to the point of collapse. Many of the people behind these excesses have shown no sense of guilt or responsibility after the fact, after the government was forced to pour billions of taxpayer dollars into their companies to keep them from going under. For these people it was just business as usual, just "the way the game is played," winner take all (or at least as much as possible), with no concern for the losers.

If we are to remain a world economic power, if we don't want the rest of the world to turn against us as a result of this arrogance, this contempt for others, the involved attitude has to change. Most of the corporate meltdowns we are referring to were driven by the same problem. People in positions of leadership, people making the important decisions, were hooked on "winning" in the old, immediate sense of the word, hooked on beating everybody else on the block.

Don't get me wrong. There is nothing wrong with winning. It is a healthy desire, a necessary desire. But when an individual, a company, or a culture becomes obsessed with winning in the short term, when no sacrifice becomes too great for those in power to do so, then the overall cost in terms of human and organization development and ultimately in terms of organization success eventually begins to outweigh the benefit. Possibly as a result of the excesses of the last decade, managers are starting to realize this. They are beginning to realize that it is important for employees to work together, to support each other's efforts so that they and the organization as a whole can achieve objectives.

But employees cannot work together effectively and accomplish their objectives unless they have been empowered (I understand—you are getting tired of hearing this word, but there is a method to my madness).

The secret, then, is to design key organization processes so that they encourage such empowerment and the resultant cooperation. We all have experienced athletic teams loaded with star players that did not do as well as expected. We all also have experienced teams composed with nonstar players or even mediocre players who did much better than expected. The difference is that the mediocre players somehow generate synergy, developing a mutual support system that encouraged the individuals to play better than they normally would have. These team demonstrated strengths that none of the individual players possessed, the additional strengths arising from the players feeding off of and contributing to each other's efforts. The whole became greater than the sum of its parts.

This should be the situation in the workplace. The major objective of individuals and units should be to do their best and to support each other's efforts. The major objective of key organization processes—the most important being the evaluation and reward system—should be to encourage such a culture. This requirement is not based on altruism. Rather, it is based on common sense, on the pragmatic realization that in almost all instances employees and units working together and supporting each other's efforts generate more profit for the company than employees doing their individual thing.

The Tie-In between Systems Theory and Ethics

The previously discussed Systems approach to organization redesign encourages the characteristics we have been talking about and leads to more ethical behavior. Most unethical acts in the workplace are committed either in the dark, when somebody gains information they believe nobody else has access to, or are committed by people who believe themselves to be above reproach. The chance for either of these situations to arise decreases greatly when an organization is truly participative, when employees have truly been empowered. It is hard to keep secrets when your fellow workers have access to anyone they need for information. It is hard to keep secrets when everybody who will be affected by a decision is asked to help shape it. Organization-wide integration, of course, also limits the chance for someone to commit an unethical act without others finding out. Too many pairs of eyes are watching, too many pairs of ears listening.

If, at the same time, the developmental part of the Systems approach is stressed, if companies treat employees as purposeful systems and try to meet their needs and desires in exchange for top-level performance that benefits everybody, loyalty and commitment are generated. A vast majority of employees do not want to behave unethically, and if the company treats them respectfully, they won't. Moreover, in a participative, integrated, rewarding culture, they will be more prone to notice the unethical behavior of others; they will be more prone to try to stop it.

The Missing Piece

All of this discussion leads us back to the missing piece mentioned earlier in the chapter in terms of improving workplace ethics—a universal standard by which to judge acts as ethical or nonethical, a standard that incorporates the strengths of the four traditional schools of ethical thought and excludes their weaknesses. The Systems approach provides this as well. The necessary standard has already been mentioned several times. It is nothing new. In fact, in terms of Western civilization Aristotle was the first to suggest it more than 2,300 years ago. The universal standard we are referring to is the *development ethic* and says that *if an act, a reward system, a training model, a decision-making approach, etc., encourages the development and effective use of positive human potential, both in terms of the individual and the workforce as a whole, it is not only good business, it is ethical.*

If any organization processes do not, however, encourage the development and effective use of positive human potential, in terms of the individual or in terms of the organization as a whole, if they encourage or force unethical behavior (an evaluation system based on the previously mentioned bell-shaped density curve, for example), then it is time for employees to start rethinking the way things are done; it is time for employees to start redesigning.

Chapter 11

Replacing the Protestant Work Ethic with the Development Ethic

It is becoming increasingly obvious that in developed countries, at least, the attitude toward work in general and toward *work ethic* specifically is changing. "People no longer understand the value of a dollar," we hear from owners and executives, "of what goes into earning one." And we hear, "It's becoming increasingly difficult to find somebody willing to give you an honest day's work for an honest day's pay, " and, "Everybody is trying to get by doing as little as possible; people have lost the work ethic."

From the other side, from workers, we hear, "The company wants me to work 50 to 60 hours a week without additional pay. That's not fair." We hear, "I worked really hard this quarter, trying to make an impression. Tom just coasted, getting out of anything that he could. And yet, he received the same salary increase that I received." We hear, "My job doesn't allow me to spend time with my wife and kids. The company even expects me to carry files home over weekends to work on."

Maybe the problem is indeed loss of the traditional work ethic. Maybe if we revive it such issues would disappear. Or, maybe, instead, the problem is that the work ethic has become obsolete and we need to find something else to build our workplace culture around, something more in tune with modern values, something that is more supportive of efforts to improve the quality of our products, our manufacturing and service processes, our management systems, our work environment, our working lives, and our lives in general.

What Exactly Is *Work*?

First of all, we need to define the concept of *work*. In any society, people spend a large portion of their time working, along with tending to family, gaining education, and participating in governance. The purpose of work in terms of society is to generate resources critical to the support of that society including wealth, buildings, transportation, education, food, healthcare, and financial services. The purpose of all these goods and services is to improve our overall quality of life.

It follows, then, that the more of its citizens' potential a society can make use of in this effort, the better off it will be. A comprehensive definition of the role of work in a society, therefore, might be *a vehicle that allows the fullest possible use of citizens' potential to continually improve the quality of life for everybody.* The companies that are currently winning and will continue to win in the local as well as the international economic arenas are the companies that work hardest to develop the potential of their employees and to use that potential in the most effective manner in terms of achieving organizational objectives.

Four types of work can be identified based on the amount of control employees have over their situation and on the amount of opportunity generated. The four types are *slave, subsistence level, situation improvement,* and *developmental.* In *slave work* individuals exercise no control over their work lives and enjoy no opportunity to benefit from their efforts. Slaves do what they are told to do on threat of punishment or even death. Frequently the only reward is survival.

People involved in *subsistence-level work* gain a small degree of control. They are paid, but just enough for the basics. They live on the edge. The work is usually repetitious and mechanical. Bosses tell them what to do and make sure they do it. They can leave their jobs but usually put themselves at great risk by doing so due to their lack of skills and their lack of savings. Most of the immigrants that swept into the United States during the late 1800s and early 1900s began with subsistence-level jobs building railroads, laboring in mines, standing on assembly lines, or sitting in textile mills.

A majority of employees today are in *situation improvement*-type jobs. These jobs pay us enough that we can continually improve our quality of life. Also, we sometimes have a say in how the work is done, though our boss still makes the final decision. While the work is frequently more challenging, it continues to be largely repetitious. Finally, once we have reached the situation improvement level, if we are dissatisfied, we can leave one job and find another. We can also return to school and receive more education so that we are qualified for a more desirable, better-paying position.

The last type of work is *developmental.* In such jobs employees have almost total control in their area of expertise. The manager becomes a facilitator, helping to generate resources, helping to integrate efforts, rather than a traditional boss who decides what is to be worked on, how the work is to be done, and by whom. Developmental work pays well in comparison. It allows those involved to continually develop and enjoy their potential. A growing number of such jobs are being generated in the fields of education and research. Entrepreneurship, the fastest-growing sector of our economy, also frequently involves developmental work in that entrepreneurs are in charge of themselves and must make all the important decisions.

Back to the Work Ethic

The work ethic was a product of the Protestant Reformation. Before that, during the Dark Ages and the medieval period, the focus was on survival; peasants worked to stay alive, usually laboring in the fields of large landowners. There was very little profit to be gained from one's efforts. The Church, at the same time, discouraged the faithful from pursuing profit, fearful that doing so would detract from the individual parishioner's quest for entrance into heaven after death and that the competition generated during the pursuit would cause the less skillful to suffer. "One just price" was set for the goods sold by craftsmen, a price that did little more than allow them to survive. This was, at best, subsistence-level work.

The most attractive reward offered during the medieval period was grace, or "points" gained toward getting into heaven. The Church encouraged parishioners to take part in "good works" beyond their normal labor. This kind of work benefited society. It included helping out at a hospice or almshouse or cathedral. While no material or "earthly" reward was expected in return for one's efforts, the payment was the points.

Next came the Renaissance period. This is when the profit motive took center stage. Due to trade deals made during the Crusades and to exploration into India, China, and Southeast Asia as well as North and South America, wealth began rolling in and profit became the rage. People realized quickly that it was the key to a better and longer life. Work was evolving, at least for the merchants and some craftsmen, from the subsistence level to the situation improvement level. But at the same time, the Church continued to condemn the quest for profit so that people were forced to make an undesirable choice. They were forced to choose between improved creature comforts in this life and their quest for salvation in the next guided by the Church.

Martin Luther to the Rescue

A way around this dilemma was found when the Protestant Reformation arrived. Martin Luther succeeded in linking all work, in linking a willingness to work hard at any profession, with getting into heaven. The previous Catholic concept of good works proclaimed that providing a service to the public, to the Church, or to the needy without asking to be paid for it helped earn God's blessing; but Luther insisted that *all* forms of work should fill this criteria, that all work contributed in a meaningful way to the advancement of society and therefore should count toward gaining God's grace. He also made profit not only acceptable but desirable in terms of salvation by proclaiming that profit was the measure of how hard one had worked and therefore the measure of how much grace one deserved.

On a more earthly level, the belief that evolved through the teachings of Luther, through common sense, and through experience was that every individual, through hard work, should be able to improve his or her situation. This, then, was the origin of the *Protestant work ethic*. The door was open now for a mass shift into situation improvement work. The Protestant Reformation and the Enlightenment period that followed allowed the middle class to come into its own.

The Paycheck Takes Center Stage

During the early Industrial Revolution, what was important in terms of the work ethic shifted rapidly from spiritual toward earthly rewards. Technology grew more complex and became the focus in the manufacturing process as employees began serving machines. Workforce responsibilities began to require less skill than those possessed by earlier craftsmen. At the same time, longer hours were necessary to meet the demands of an increasingly competitive marketplace that sought an expanding range of products. The work ethic evolved into a willingness to sacrifice 12–14 hours a day at a repetitive task that was deadening intellectually and spiritually to receive a paycheck that allowed one to survive.

During the early Industrial Revolution, slave-type work was not uncommon. Child employees were sometimes chained to their machines. Employees were so deeply in debt to their employers because they were forced to live in relatively expensive company housing and to buy whatever they needed from the company store that they could not quit and, in many cases, were literally worked to death.

Most employees during the early Industrial Revolution were trapped at the subsistence level. Fairly rapidly, however, due to intervention by newly formed unions and eventually by the federal government, the workforce moved to the situation improvement level, salaries provided more buying power, and employees gained a steadily increasing amount of control over their working lives. But bosses still made the decisions, most jobs were still repetitive and nondevelopmental, and the work ethic still remained the guiding principle. Employees sacrificed a majority of their weekdays completing nondevelopmental tasks to earn a paycheck that allowed them and their families to pursue developmental as well as pleasurable activities during nonworking hours.

Still Not Good Enough

While this was a great improvement, the workforce again eventually grew dissatisfied. Earning money and making an adequate salary was important to improving one's quality of life, yes, but wasting a lot of time on nondevelopmental activities to do so didn't make sense, especially as the level of education rose among the workforce. Employees began demanding more. They wanted challenge in their jobs, they wanted the authority to make decisions they were capable of making and to solve problems they were capable of solving. They wanted to be listened to when they came up with new ideas. In sum, they sought the right to develop their potential as a means of improving their quality of life during working hours as well as during nonworking hours.

The work ethic as a primary vehicle for spurring productivity obviously didn't work so well anymore. One alternative was to try to modify it so that it fit into the evolving workplace culture. But how should it be modified? Religion no longer played an important role in the equation; very few still regarded hard work as a means of gaining grace. Also, the more pragmatic belief that "the harder one works, the more one should benefit economically" no longer rang true, if ever it had. Experience showed us that the willingness to work hard was not the only important criterion for improving one's salary. Some of those who worked the hardest, in fact, gained the least in terms of rewards.

Perhaps the work ethic was simply worn out; what value it once did possess now withered to the point where it could not be revived. Perhaps, the time of the work ethic had passed and it should be laid to rest, with a replacement discovered that would help revitalize the world of work.

Development Ethic as an Alternative

A growing number of people are beginning to realize that the development ethic introduced in the last chapter as the standard by which to judge ethical behavior can also serve as a replacement for the work ethic. And why not? It makes sense. Beliefs concerning ethics have always played a large role in the way companies are run and in the way employees are expected to work.

If the development ethic does indeed become a foundational cornerstone of our society, it can certainly serve more than one purpose. An approach to defining the meaning of life, this ethic, as we said, was first introduced to Western society by the Greek philosopher Aristotle. It has popped up periodically throughout history, most recently being revived and modified slightly to better fit our modern age by practitioners of the Systems school of management theory.

The development ethic says that the purpose of life is to develop and enjoy our positive human potential to the fullest possible extent, and then to turn around and use that potential to help others develop and enjoy theirs. In order for us to develop our individual potential, society must assist by providing *five critical inputs*—wealth, education, good governance, an environment that encourages development, and time.

The first input required is the *wealth* needed to support development-related activities. Society is responsible for ensuring that all citizens have access to jobs that provide a decent salary. Wealth, more than the other inputs, is foundational to development. Without a strong economy, it would be more difficult for a society to generate the other required inputs. But while the most recent version of the work ethic says wealth is the *only* important input, the development ethic disagrees strongly.

The second input critical to our quest is access to *education*. The involved education system should be affordable to everybody and should focus on realizing individual potential more so than on hammering students into predetermined molds. An increasing number of companies understand the value of offering the opportunity for ongoing education to their employees at all levels.

The third input required from society is a *system of governance* in the workplace, the community, and the nation that encourages citizens to pursue self-development and that facilitates their efforts. Democracy, when it is working properly, is the best of all possible systems for this purpose.

The fourth input required of society is *an environment both in the community and the workplace that supports development-related activities*. It is hard to work on developing one's potential when there is constant noise, when cigarette smoke fills the air, when one is worried about being downsized or about young children returning home from school to an empty house. The ideal environment for development is one that stimulates, but in a positive way, while at the same time soothing the individual. The ideal environment is one that a person has control over. This means that in the office, for example, employees should have a say in how their space is organized and decorated.

And, finally, the fifth societal input must be *time*. Society should help ensure that we have sufficient time to do the things necessary to develop our positive potential. If we spend a majority of our waking hours in the office focused solely on making more money, as is the trend in the United States, we don't have enough left to pursue other developmental activities, both in the office and outside.

These are the five inputs that society and employers should provide so that people can develop their potential. And once they have done so, employees who have benefited are expected to use that potential to help generate more of the inputs for others to take advantage of and to dedicate their enhanced talents to improvement of the company's fortunes as well as those of society in general. This agreement creates a win-win-win situation. The individual obviously wins. The company wins. Society wins.

Development Ethic Generates Commitment to Improved Productivity

Chapter 1 mentioned the amount of time spent on nondevelopmental, mind-dulling work in factories and offices during the Industrial Revolution. Today's trend is toward finding ways to replace those activities with developmental ones. Our best friend in facing this challenge is, of course, the technology that is taking over repetitive, mind-numbing tasks so that employees can move on to more challenging ones such as planning, product development, and work design.

In terms of our now critical focus on continually improving the quality of products, manufacturing and service processes, management systems, and the work environment, the changeover is imperative. The work ethic was built around individual performance rather than team performance. The work ethic taught that the best employees are those who excel in obeying superiors, in doing what they are told to do. The work ethic believed strongly in the hierarchy, in drawing a clear line between those who make decisions and those responsible for implementing them. The work ethic focused on predefined job responsibilities. Personal matters such as self-development should be attended to during nonworking hours.

On the other hand, as we have eventually learned, the driving force behind improved productivity is *employee commitment*. When the workforce is committed, it will take care of the rest. We have also learned that *respect* is key to gaining employee commitment and that there is no better way to show respect for your employees than to encourage them to develop their potential, to facilitate these efforts, and to reward employees for doing so.

Workers in progressive companies are no longer expected to follow the dictates of the now outdated work ethic in order to accomplish what they are programmed to accomplish as parts of a "well-oiled machine." Rather, they are increasingly being expected to make decisions, solve problems, enhance their education level, design their own work, and train each other. These activities, while increasing productivity, also feed right into the development ethic, generating again a win-win situation. The employee gains more than just a salary from work, with individual development occurring simultaneously and continuously. The company benefits from the employees' enhanced skills and growing enthusiasm.

It Is Time for a Change

It is becoming increasingly apparent that the work ethic no longer suffices and that the development ethic makes more sense in the modern-day world of work. A growing number of business leaders have begun to agree with these sentiments. The time for change has arrived. The work ethic has run out of steam. The development ethic is needed to encourage and drive future, ongoing efforts to improve our productivity, our economy, and our society.

Chapter 12

Training for the Modern Age

Now it is time to address training, about which, up to this point, we have not said many positive things. And we have not done so with good reason because (and here it comes, another one of those heavy statements) *the way most current approaches to training are designed does not produce the best possible results. Employees do not get what they could and should get from the involved activities. Too frequently they absorb little that is relevant to their work, little that will help improve their performance. Frequently, the main challenge they have to deal with during training sessions is staying awake.*

We need to make clear at this point that the failings we are talking about are not due to lack of effort on the part of those responsible for organizing and delivering the training. They are usually due, rather, to faults in the training model adopted. Quite simply, most such models do not get those being trained involved in the most effective manner.

Getting Down to It with Empowerment

One of the currently popular concepts in modern-day executive circles is the concept of *empowerment,* which plays such a key role in the message being delivered through *Out of the Box Thinking for Successful Managers.* Empowerment is being pushed in both the private and public sectors, frequently with good results. At the same time, however, though the results are good, they are not as good as they could, or should, be. The reason is that though empowerment sounds like a simple process, it can be more demanding than most suspect.

There are actually four levels of empowerment. The first is traditional bossism: "I tell you what to do; then I empower you to do it." The second level is, "I want you to give me your input concerning how we should handle this project; then I will decide whether or not to take what you offer into account as I define the steps that are necessary and decide who should take them." The third level is, "I want you, John, or you guys as a team to decide what should be done and how to do it. But once you make these decisions, you must get my approval before acting, and I of course retain the right to veto anything I find questionable." Finally, the fourth level is, "These are the results we are looking for. How we achieve them is up to you people. You decide what needs to be done and who will do it. You make the decisions. I will function as a resource and as an on-call facilitator." Level four, or "real" empowerment, centers on turning both authority and responsibility over to employees in their areas of expertise, and then showing a willingness to support their efforts.

The central argument of this chapter, therefore, is that while we currently spend quite a bit of time and money training managers how to empower their reports, most of what they are being given does not produce the desired results because most of what they are being given leaves the manager in charge of the process (level one, two, or three empowerment) rather than the employees. What we are saying is that

empowerment needs to *begin with* the training process, not
follow it. What we are saying is that *a more effective approach
to all types of training, in that all types have to do directly
or indirectly with empowerment, would be to skip directly to
the employees, to allow them to train themselves concerning
empowerment and other things, this attitude, in itself, encouraging empowerment.*

But, Hey, It Still Works Pretty Well

Before going any further with this thought, let's look at the traditional approach to training and see how empowering it actually is. The involved training can be either informal or formal.
By informal we can mean learning by the seat of our pants,
diving in immediately with almost no guidance, and asking
a lot of questions as a way of finding out what we need to
find out to survive. By informal training we can also mean
shadowing somebody with the knowledge and skills sought,
or, perhaps serving as an apprentice or intern. These types of
training most frequently occur when new hires are involved.

By formal training we mean classroom sessions headed by
a member of the training department or by a consultant. We
can also mean training delivered by computer programs, being
assigned a program to study or picking one that interests us
to learn from. These types of training most frequently involve
employees who have been with the company for a while and
are trying to upgrade skills or to improve their work-related
knowledge base.

The training function has traditionally been a responsibility
of the human resources department. The person in charge of
training has participated in the organization's long-range planning effort or at least has been given access to the organization's objectives for the following year as defined by upper-level
management. That person has then sat down either alone or
with reports and identified the types of training necessary to

support achievement of the organization's long-range objectives, frequently with input from the heads of other departments.

The next step has been to identify the resources required to provide the desired training in terms of personnel, technology, and computer programs. Next, a training schedule has been negotiated with the heads of departments. This schedule includes when and where the training will take place and whether classroom space or computer labs need to be reserved. Finally, the training begins.

In terms of empowerment, *informal training* ("Do as I say, but at the same time, you can ask questions") is necessary because the people receiving the training know so little at this point in their careers. *Formal training*, however, has also traditionally been, "Do as I say," when it should not be. During formal training, while those in the class and those on the computer are encouraged to participate through role playing, scenario building, swapping viewpoints, and other exercises, they are not participating in a manner that leads to full empowerment. During the exercise they are encouraged to speak out, and their opinions and questions are considered and responded to by the trainer, but that person is still in charge, still shaping and driving the agenda, rather than the trainees being in charge, which gives the exercise a level two or level three flavor of empowerment at best.

But How Do We Change This Scenario?

Because training begins with identification of the organization's long-term objectives, one would think that top-level management has a pretty good idea of what new skills need to be learned and what old skills should be updated. Quite frequently this is true. But the human resources department and the managers from other functions included in the process of identifying skills to be worked on are doing so with a top-down perspective rather than bottom-up, and this usually leaves out a lot of issues that might be important to success. It also frequently stresses the wrong things. The top-down interpretation of and reaction to each unit's situation is usually quite different from that of the people who are in the trenches, the ones actually producing the goods and delivering the services.

For example, a telephone sales company's executives might decide that a need exists to train employees to work faster so as to increase sales, while the employees themselves believe that the problem is actually one of burnout and that to increase sales they need training in how to avoid burnout.

The employees behind the desks or operating the machines or servicing the customer directly are those who understand best why they are having trouble meeting quotas or deadlines, why customers are complaining, why there is so much employee turnover, why so many mistakes are being made during the inventory process. It is often the case as well that employees, having lived with these situations and problems on a daily basis, harbor a pretty good idea of what kind of training is needed to eliminate these problems.

When in-house trainers or consultants show up and claim to understand the situation or to have been told by bosses what the problem is and then begin the "necessary" training without any real input from those most affected, the major result can be frustration. Sitting through such sessions can be a real morale killer.

To get the best results, employees need, as we have said, to be involved in training from the start. Once they are informed of the organization's long-term objectives by their boss, these things having come down through the hierarchy, they should be asked for their opinions as to what types of training would help facilitate achievement of those objectives.

This can be done individually, in a meeting, or through a survey. It can also be done through formation of a committee including representatives from all parts of the organization that meets periodically to identify training needs. The next requirement in this instance would be for the committee to prioritize these needs based on the organization's long-term objectives and on input from upper-level management. After that, committee members could design the actual training modules required to meet these needs. A subcommittee could be formed to design each module, the subcommittee including anybody in the organization and even participants from outside who committee members think could contribute meaningfully. Next, the committee could decide who should deliver each training module, using employees with the appropriate experience when possible, but also bringing in experts from outside the company when necessary. Finally, the committee could gather feedback on the training sessions that the employees have given directly to their committee representative, and use this feedback to improve the modules.

It Really Does Make Sense, and Saves Money to Boot

A growing number of companies that are moving toward increased employee involvement have reached or are approaching levels two and three of empowerment. Those with the most experience in such companies help identify training needs and help design and deliver the actual training. One of the major benefits is cost. A September 29, 2002, article in the *Chicago Tribune* cited a small Florida public relations and marketing firm named Thorp & Co. that cut the cost of individual employee training from $6,000 per year to $4,800 by keeping the training in-house using volunteers from the workforce. Owner Patricia Thorp was quoted as saying that the in-house trainers do a better job of "giving employees the skills they need."

For companies that have a training group already in place as part of their human resources department, by instituting the employee participation model you now have maybe 100 people capable of delivering courses rather than 3 or 4, and the role of training group members changes to facilitators. Their main responsibility will now be to help train the trainers, to instruct them in delivery techniques, to critique their performance, to make sure they have access to necessary resources. The savings in terms of expediency alone should be obvious.

In organizations practicing level four empowerment, because they have been given ownership of the process, employees will be more likely to take the training seriously, to make sure it covers the necessary topics, and to critique it continually instead of waiting till afterward to fill out their evaluations.

This is not to say that senior management should never be able to mandate training. There are situations where senior management definitely should lay out what is required. An example would be when a new technology is introduced, or a new product added to the mix, or a new region opened, or a new customer population sought after. Senior management should send down what is needed, but lower-level employees should be asked for input as well.

All Sorts of Benefits, Big and Small

Some advantages of this approach are obvious. Others are more subtle, such as the enhanced level of integration resulting from it. Again, most traditional training models fall short. They do so because the integration is designed and orchestrated from higher levels that have a limited idea of what is going on below, the effect their directives have on those who must deal with the results. Sometimes this approach works; but why take a chance? Why not have representatives from all units (not managers) meet and compare their training needs and resources to discover where they overlap, where the training designed for one unit might affect that designed for another, and where combining efforts might be of advantage? The fact that lower-level employees meet on a regular basis to compare notes helps ensure organization-wide integration.

Another more subtle advantage is that level four empowerment helps ensure that the training effort will be ongoing and flexible. Instead of one or a few people in the training department trying to keep up with changes in organization operations and in the market environment that might necessitate shifts in their offerings, the trainees themselves meet on a regular basis to compare notes on what is happening both in their areas of expertise and in the marketplace, integrating this information, then deciding what changes to their training schedule might be advisable. These people, of course, will have conferred with their immediate workplace peers to gather suggestions before coming to the meeting and will carry any proposed change back for critique. If somebody comes up with a valid concern, the group can assemble again to discuss it.

Finally, in terms of more subtle advantages, the degree of learning will increase when level four empowerment is applied to training. It has eventually been recognized in the business world that the more that employees contribute to the shaping of a project, be it the development of a new product or the design of the training effort, the more they are going to learn from that project. In this case we are talking not only about the identification of training needs but also about the design of the presentation format, the delivery of information, and the critique of both design and delivery. Those involved most fully in this effort will be learning about the training process, they will be doing research on topics and on how the information should be delivered, they will be learning about the organization's strengths and weaknesses, about how organization systems interact.

Upper-level management's main role would be to monitor the committee's decisions and to support its efforts. Members of upper-level management would be invited to committee meetings on an as-needed basis to help define training needs, define priorities, and generate resources.

In summation, the more that employees are involved in all phases of the training process—identification of needs, design and delivery of the training, critique of what was delivered— the more the company as a whole is going to benefit.

Chapter 13

Is a Better Approach to Improving Safety Possible?

Though the issue discussed in this chapter in possibly not as world changing as those addressed in earlier ones, it is still important. This chapter is about our traditional approach to safety programs. Quite simply, that approach is not as effective as it could be. The major problem, once again, is not that those putting together and presenting the material are slacking off. Rather, it is the way the material and presentation are designed.

Safety programs began for two reasons. The first, which resulted largely from union efforts, was to improve the quality of employees' working lives. The second, which was and is mainly management driven, was to improve profits by cutting down on the cost of injuries in terms of medical expenses, insurance, and lost time.

To date, millions of dollars have been spent on efforts to improve safety in the workplace. But have these millions of dollars produced the desired results? It is the author's opinion that, in too many cases, they have not. Due to the way many safety programs are organized, they are in fact frequently a waste of time and money. At the same time, they do not enhance the quality of employees' working lives. In extreme cases, they adversely affect employee morale and, thus, at least indirectly, adversely affect productivity and profits.

Here's How It's Done and What's Wrong with the Approach

A typical safety program includes the following elements:

■ Posters and other educational materials
■ Presentations on safety issues as a reminder of things employees should already know and as a warning of new dangers in the workplace
■ Periodic unit meetings to pinpoint local safety issues and sometimes to define precautions and/or solutions
■ Accident reports, monthly records of lost-time and non-lost-time accidents
■ A head of safety at the facility level responsible for overseeing all of the above
■ A corporate safety director responsible for coordinating the education program and for reducing accidents on a corporate-wide basis

Several problems are associated with this approach, including the following:

1. Lack of ownership of the program by those most important to its success
2. Absence of an effective "vehicle" for instituting safety-related changes in the workplace
3. Dependence on a reward system designed in such a way that it can actually hamper efforts to make the workplace safer

Looking at the ownership problem, while employees and employee safety committees are sometimes allowed to identify problems, it is usually management that defines and implements the desired changes. Employees, therefore, do not make the contribution they are capable of making. Members of the workforce would be more likely to stress safety if they had the power to implement changes they thought necessary. This approach makes sense for several reasons.

First, workers, more than managers in most situations, know what safety problems exist because they are forced to deal with them on a daily basis. They also frequently know appropriate solutions to these problems for the same reason.

Second, because there are more workers than managers, if given the necessary authority and access to the necessary resources, the workers can deal with more problems in a shorter period of time.

Third, lower-level managers usually have a wider range of responsibilities than workers, safety improvement being just one. They also frequently have a different set of priorities so that safety issues important to the workers sometimes take a backseat.

Finally, when workers gain ownership to improvements by contributing to them, a number of steps in the correction process are eliminated and proper feedback is ensured. As a result, the chances for a foul-up in communication or for a work order to get lost are reduced.

Very few organizations have put into place a suitable vehicle for implementing safety-related changes in the workplace. Projects tend to compete for attention on all levels. Individual employees or small groups bring competing safety issues to managers. Managers, in turn, bring their competing lists to the maintenance department, which combines them with lists from other sources and tries to decide which projects to schedule first. Safety projects involving a production process breakdown and those submitted by top-level management are given priority for obvious reasons. Others funneling upward, unless there is a crisis, usually must wait.

Getting beyond the Hustle

In terms of incentives, emphasis has traditionally been on reducing the number of accidents, the key word here being *number.* As a result of this approach, the corporate safety director is graded on how effectively he or she has cut the number of accidents reported, the key word here being *reported.* Such reductions occur in three ways: by luck, by legitimate educational efforts, or by illegitimate maneuvering.

The term *illegitimate maneuvering* refers to attempts to misrepresent reality. One way of doing this is by simply fudging the numbers. An extreme example of such fudging would be to consider an accident as reportable only when the victim is carried out on a stretcher. Another, not-so-extreme example that I heard about was to give an employee who injured his leg during working hours the job of monitoring the infirmary waiting room television until he was able to return to normal duties so that no lost time needed to be reported.

A second, more subtle strategy is for the corporate safety director to let it be known that accident rates are expected to decrease and that managers' performance evaluations could be adversely affected if they do not. As a result, workers frequently are forced to ignore injuries or to stock their lockers with medical supplies. If an injury is too serious to tend to in this manner, an excuse is found for the employee to go home early or to a hospital, with co-workers covering in his or her absence.

A third approach is to punish the worker who goes to the infirmary, making that person fill out a long accident report, investigating the accident to discover to what degree negligence was the cause, and broadcasting the injured worker's name along with an account of his or her "crime."

Because the current reward system stresses putting together a record number of accident-free days, because its focus is, once again, on the numbers, safety programs often alienate the very people whose quality of working life and productivity they are supposed to improve. Because of this quantitative rather than qualitative approach, employees become victims, not beneficiaries of such efforts.

Another Way to Deal with Safety Issues

There is a need to give safety-related recommendations submitted by lower-level employees more of a chance to make an impact. One way is to set up a vehicle that encourages departmental or unit consensus on safety project priorities. Thus, a sizable portion of the unit workforce would be involved in making a request for action, rather than just one individual or several individuals. A network of quality improvement teams can provide such a vehicle, or a network of teams focused solely on safety issues, these latter teams meeting on an as-needed basis. The most important characteristic possessed by both alternatives is that, by definition, they allow team members to control all phases of safety-related projects in their areas of expertise. Also, both alternatives would be governed by the same set of quality improvement process ground rules discussed in Chapter 5. These rules encourage, for one thing, integration of safety-related suggestions and decisions on an organization-wide basis.

I would also suggest the following additional ways to make an organization safety program more effective. To start with, and perhaps most importantly, top-level management should not keep track of or periodically broadcast the number of accidents that have occurred, at least not organization-wide. Such a practice puts emphasis in the wrong place.

The safety director should function mainly as a resource, meeting the safety-related requests of teams in the network as the teams identify and deal with unit needs. The safety director should also help coordinate efforts. An example is that if two teams were working on the same issue and requested the same type of training for their unit members, the director could arrange one joint session instead of two. Also, the safety director should make sure that top-level management is kept abreast of developments and that it continues to demonstrate highly visible support for the program.

When employees are injured, the process of seeking treatment should be made as painless as possible. The only reports required should be those filled out by the medical staff for insurance purposes.

A record of the number and types of accidents that occur should be kept at the unit level as a means of helping to pinpoint trouble areas, but not as a measure of individual performance. The safety director should have access to these records for the purposes of identifying trends, defining trouble spots from an organization-wide perspective, and identifying resources required to deal with issues. These records should in no way influence any employee's performance evaluation. The only time they should be taken into account is when an employee is applying for a job-related disability.

Worth a Try?

If these suggestions are put into place, the belief is that the effectiveness of safety programs will increase. Safety will no longer be something that is done to the workers or is taught to them by management. It will become something that workers teach themselves, oversee, and ensure. It will become part of their everyday activities, a self-defined job responsibility. Efforts to improve safety will, in effect, become a part of their everyday workplace culture.

Chapter 14

Unions: From Leadership to Playing Catch-Up

A lot of the people who read this book will be anti-union. They are the people who wish unions would go away, just disappear or be made illegal so that companies can conduct their business in the most efficient manner, keeping employees on a tight rein and pointed in the right direction.

These people would be wrong.

Unions are absolutely necessary in any culture that believes in a balance of powers. Every developed country in the world has unions of some sort representing their workforce. The major difference between the United States and other countries is that in other countries, unions and management more so have learned to work together, realizing that constant confrontation hurts productivity so that everybody—both management and labor—suffers. There are, of course, still disputes in these other countries, even strikes. But not as many as in the United States, as serious efforts are made on both sides to avoid them, to resolve differences before they become detrimental to the bottom line.

To facilitate the resolution of differences, large organizations in most Western European countries have instituted labor-management councils. These councils usually meet on a monthly basis, where representatives of the workers, most often union officials, sit down with representatives of upper-level management to discuss new company projects, shifts in policy, the economy, and other more global topics, with management taking the lead. They also discuss work or office floor problems, with labor representatives taking the lead. The objective is to arrive at decisions acceptable to both sides and to find solutions to employee problems before they escalate into grievances.

Birth and Rebirth of the Union Movement in the United States

Unions began to gain a foothold in the United States during the late 1800s. At that point in history the economy was dominated by a group of some 20 "robber barons" who bragged about "owning" state and national politicians. Up to 30 percent of the workforce was unemployed during this period. There was a serious recession approximately every 10 years. Fourteen-hour workdays were not uncommon. Child labor was rampant. Workers had no safety net—no pension, no health-care benefits, no way to appeal unjust treatment.

Concerning the wealth of the nation, the middle class was very small. There were only the owners, who were very rich, pouring into their coffers a steadily increasing share of the wealth generated; and the poor working class, who lived basically in survival mode with little or no chance to improve their circumstances and generate a better opportunity for their children.

"Couldn't happen today," I hear. "Too much has changed."

Well, anybody who says that it "couldn't happen today" hasn't been paying attention. The gap between the very wealthy and the rest of us is, once again, widening steadily. Wall Street and the banking industry are, once again, out of control. Concerning politics, instead of directly buying politicians with bribes as in the old days, obscene amounts of money are being contributed to buy elections, the data showing that in most instances the politician who has the most to spend normally wins. And from where do politicians gather the necessary campaign donations?

So, how do we stop this destructive cycle? Unions, with a lot of help from President Theodore Roosevelt, stopped it the first time around. Unions obviously should be the natural weapon of choice this time also. But unions are not very popular at the moment, and for good reason. In order to make the necessary impact, they must first get their own act in order.

Those condemning unions are not totally wrong. Many of the faults being pointed out can be documented. One might suspect, however, that what critics are condemning is not so much the concept of unionization as it is the things unions currently are focusing on, the outdated practices that many of them cling to. Workers still need protection from exploitation. Such protection benefits not only the worker but has a positive effect on productivity as well. I don't think that most people in the modern world of work would argue with that statement.

There is, of course, actually a way to get rid of unions while, at the same time, protecting workers, thus creating a win-win situation. That way would be to adopt the management model presented in Chapter 9. Workforce representatives sitting on Circular Organization level boards would be able to protect their interests while helping make the important decisions. The three-tiered reward system would tie everybody's pay to their productivity and stop upper-level managers from overcompensating themselves. Union officials, in this instance, would no longer be needed to represent employee interests. The employees themselves would have gained the authority to do so.

In actuality, however, there is very little chance of organizations adopting this model in the near future. Too many people on both the union and management sides would be threatened by it. The immediate challenge facing us, therefore, is to help make current-day unions more effective, to reestablish their caretaking role in society.

Why Unions Began to Lose Their Clout

Unions have traditionally led the way toward an improved quality of working life. Historically they have played a major role in securing the 40-hour workweek; introducing child labor laws; passing the minimum wage act; gaining protection from injury and harassment; and expanding fringe benefits such as healthcare, vacation time, sick leave, and pensions. But in modern times and in terms of workplace advancements necessary for the United States to maintain its leadership role in the global economy, unions have too frequently lagged behind management, sometimes even attempting to thwart the necessary innovations.

Several reasons can be cited for the hesitancy and caution of union leaders. One is that though such leaders have much to gain in the long run, they are more at risk than top-level managers. Specifically, CEOs and other senior executives can fake their commitment to employees' receiving more say in the decision-making process. They can throw around the appropriate buzzwords; they can spend lots of money on training and consultants while at the same time refusing to change their own management style in ways important to the success of the necessary cultural shift.

In essence, CEOs can focus on presenting an image of increased employee involvement while avoiding the necessary "content" and get away with it, at least in the short run. Too many of them remain committed to the traditional definition of employee empowerment, "I tell you what to do and then empower you to do it." The workforce has little leverage, even when top management's lack of commitment becomes obvious. At the same time, board members and stockholders are too far removed to properly evaluate actions and intentions. The hype and the bottom line are all they see, and the bottom line can be manipulated, as we have witnessed in too many recent scandals.

Union leaders, on the other hand, are directly responsible to and dependent upon those most deeply affected by the work-life changes being advocated. They must be sure that worker empowerment is not just another management ploy to reduce the union's say. At the same time they must deal with the hard and often threatening realization that the dream their movement was built around might actually be coming true.

Where the Real Battle Lies

Unions were formed initially around three basic issues— worker pay, job security, and workplace safety. The underlying purpose from which these issues sprang, the underlying purpose of the demands made by union leaders, of the often bloody strikes used to cut into owners' profits and to force them to the bargaining table, was to give employees increased power over their working lives, increased power to improve those lives.

In the modern-day workplace the desired transition is indeed occurring, though very slowly. A growing number of companies are realizing that winning the global competition no longer depends on who has the most money to invest. The financial world is awash with money. It no longer depends on who has the most advanced technology. Henry Ford's moving assembly line allowed him an advantage for nearly 20 years; but with the advent of reverse engineering, new innovations can now be deciphered and even improved upon in a matter of weeks or months. It no longer depends on who is able to gain access to valuable information and how quickly they can do so. Now the major challenge concerning information is filtering the overload flowing in.

Winning the global competition today depends mainly on who makes the most effective use of employee expertise and has developed the best procedures for finding good employees, training them well, facilitating their efforts, rewarding them adequately, and holding on to them. This is currently the key. As a result, progressive companies are beginning to offer more reasonable salary levels, profit-sharing plans, good benefits packages that the employees can help shape, and innovations such as flex time and telecommuting. Progressive companies are playing down competition between employees and encouraging the team approach as the best way to improve productivity so that everybody benefits.

Of course there are holdouts, Walmart and McDonald's for example—companies that still support the Adam Smith/ Frederick Taylor approach, companies that continue to break the production or service delivery process down into its simplest possible parts so that employees don't need much training and don't need to think as they repeat the same action or calculation over and over. Smith introduced this approach during the 1700s to make unskilled peasants employable so that they could earn a wage and feed their families, and Taylor improved on it in the early 1900s to increase the efficiency of production so that the extra wealth generated could be distributed in an equitable manner; however, our current holdouts continue to practice the "economic man" philosophy made popular during the early Industrial Revolution. Their desire remains to get the most out of their employees for the least possible reward. If the employees quit, fine, because little if anything has been invested and a line of applicants is waiting at the door.

Another indication of this lingering "economic man" mentality is the tendency of the holdouts to reward themselves as much of the wealth generated as possible so that while low-level workers are earning close to minimum wage, the earnings of top-level executives often amount to millions annually, no matter how well or how poorly their company fares. In Western European countries, whose citizens are considered to enjoy an overall quality of life superior to that of US citizens, the worker-to-CEO salary ratio for most firms lies between 1:10 and 1:20 (lowest to highest) while in the United States it has been estimated to be as high as 1:500 and is still climbing. The people earning this kind of wage obviously don't need all that money. Rather, it serves mainly to make an impression. One might suspect that a competition rages to see who can post the largest number among those who constitute the pay-scale elite. It also is used to "buy" political favor so that laws similar to those in European countries that limit the compensation received by stock brokers, bankers, and corporate executives are not passed.

So, how do we stop this unfair distribution of the wealth generated? Unions are perhaps the only vehicle in existence today with any chance of changing the situation, with any chance of getting our modern-day robber barons under control. But in order to take on the holdouts successfully, unions first need to reinvent themselves, to rethink their mission.

Too Much Focus on Local Issues?

The major power of early unions rested in the number of people represented, the number of people supporting their efforts. That has traditionally been the foundational strength of unions, much more so than political connections or contributions to campaigns or friends in the media. Depending on the sheer voting power of numbers, unions were able to force change. But the percentage of the workforce unionized has shrunk steadily since the mid-1900s. Recent estimations put it at around 10 percent of the workforce.

At least part of the reason for this decline is that unions have become increasingly focused on what we will call local issues. When they were first formed in the United States during the second half of the nineteenth century, they addressed global issues that affected all workers, both skilled and unskilled. Shop or office floor issues were also important, but the global ones that affected every employee were the glue that held the movement together and made it attractive. Today, however, most of those global issues, largely through the efforts of unions, have been dealt with, or at least models have been generated for dealing with them if companies are willing.

Unions, as a result of this progress, have concentrated increasingly on local issues, on issues that affect union members in individual companies. They have become buried in the details of their particular situation. When regional or national leaders try to start a movement, the first question is, What affect will this have on members of our local? Though this perspective is understandable, it is about as far away as we can get from, What effect will this movement have on all union members nationally and, more importantly, on our company's total workforce, on the national workforce as a whole?

Another problem with this loss of a global perspective is that the union culture has become *us against them*, but not us against *management* so much as us against *non-union workers*. Union members generally receive 10–30 percent more pay than non-union workers and negotiate for workplace improvement not available to non-union employees. The higher pay and improvements are certainly deserved, but the idea that they are available only to the unionized part of the workforce creates resentment. Say a business needs two skill sets. The part of the workforce with one is unionized; the part of the workforce with the other is not. Though the amount of work required is roughly equivalent, the union employees earn more. Because of this they are forced to spend time defending their advantage against those who think it is unfair.

This situation makes no sense at all if the ultimate objective is to gain the clout necessary to continue forcing desired workplace improvements, to have a say in such things as executive compensation. It is like an army with two divisions where the divisions start fighting each other rather than joining forces to attack the enemy.

Another thing aggravating this confrontation is the right-to-work movement. Non-union workers believe they have the right to work in unionized offices and shops without having to join and pay dues. Union members believe such people are taking advantage of the situation, gaining at least some of the benefits union leaders bargain for without having to pay the price of membership. Again, the right-to-work issue is a local battle mired in local politics. It is also a losing cause for the union movement if increasing membership is a first step toward regaining the power necessary to achieve global objectives. Any effort to force people to join a union is a mistake. Unions have to find ways to make them *want* to join.

Our modern-day robber barons, of course, are fully cognizant of the union sector's current dilemma and work to reinforce it, to keep unions on the defensive, to keep them occupied with the struggle to retain the remaining benefits enjoyed by their remaining members so that they do not have time to think about the big picture, to start developing the perspective necessary to rebuild. Quite simply, the robber barons are winning in their effort to wipe out the union movement. If they succeed, the results will probably be disastrous. They will again buy off government as they did in the late 1800s and early 1900s. Employees will have no protector, the middle class will continue to shrink, and the gap between the very wealthy and the rest of us will continue to widen.

This, of course, cannot be allowed to happen; for as we know, the middle class is the backbone of any healthy economy and unions help protect it. Without a middle class the United States will most likely deteriorate into a third-world country.

Need for Universal Healthcare as a Starting Point

In the realm of marketing theory, there are two major strategies: push and pull. Push is when a store goes out and tries to convince potential customers that what it has to offer is of value to them through advertising and such. Pull includes efforts to draw customers into the store by having reduced-price sales, having two-for-one offers, and making coupons available.

During their prime, unions concentrated on pushing the desirability of what they had to offer out into the public. This included movement toward reasonable wages, job security, and a safer workplace. Today, however, their emphasis is mainly on a pull strategy: "See the benefits you will gain by unionizing your company? Come to us." But pull is obviously not working that well, as the steady decrease in union membership indicates. Too frequently, as has been said, it incites resentment rather than interest.

Unions need to return to their initial push approach. They need to focus on global issues that will unify workers from different economic sectors and arouse in them the desire to find effective leadership. There is one issue that would provide a good starting point in this shift back toward the global; this issue greatly affects both union and non-union workers, and it could give all workers a common goal, with the union movement taking the lead as an organizing agent: It is our nation's need for universal healthcare.

The United States is the only developed country in the world lacking some form of universal care. Millions of US citizens live without insurance or suffer from inadequate coverage. The per capita cost for healthcare services in the United States is double that of any other nation. At the same time, the United States is the only country where insurance companies continue to take approximately one-third of every dollar spent on healthcare for administrative expenses. Pharmaceuticals in more progressive countries, if they are not free, cost roughly half as much as those in the United States. The 2000 World Health Organization ranked the United States 38th in terms of overall healthcare provision, even behind several developing countries—and that position has not changed much in more recent years.

Why does this situation continue? It continues because the lobbies for traditional healthcare institutions, for insurers, and for the pharmaceutical industry are among the strongest in Washington, spending millions of dollars on legislators' campaigns in return for their votes. Obamacare has made some inroads, but the first thing stripped from the president's bill was the part introducing a universal system. Also, Obamacare leaves insurance companies as a middleman in every transaction.

So far no organization with real clout has stood up to those who continue to treat the US healthcare system as a cash cow. The union movement could take on this role; it should take on this role and make the fight for a universal healthcare system one of its global issues, representing all US families, not just those who belong to unions. Such a move would doubtlessly make unions more attractive to non-union employees.

Out-of-Control Executive Compensation as a Second Focus

Universal healthcare could be a warm-up. But two major global issues the union movement should address are the absurd compensation packages top executives in many companies award themselves and the growing threat that technology poses to traditional jobs.

Paul Krugman, in his "Opinion Pages" editorial entitled "Robots and Robber Barons" (*The New York Times*, December 9, 2012), hit the nail squarely on the head concerning compensation. He said that while corporate profits are rising, little if any of the new wealth is filtering down and salary levels remain stagnant no matter how well educated or trained employees are, no matter how productive they are. The additional profits are being absorbed by the top levels of management.

This issue would give union and non-union workers another common goal, one they all consider important, one they could work toward together. Unions could provide the necessary platform from which to launch a well-integrated effort to get executive compensation under control. Unions could provide the resources necessary to support an effective public education campaign. Unions could encourage contacts in Congress to introduce the necessary legislation. Unions could make executive compensation an issue during the election cycle. Unions could take the lead in raising the money needed to support such efforts. A battery of union lawyers would be available to help protect those leading the attack as well as employees who draw the ire of bosses.

One possible platform theme, one possible approach around which compensation-controlling legislation can be developed, a theme that would definitely attract attention, comes from Europe, where in some nations the previously mentioned required ratio between the highest and lowest pay levels is defined by law. No, this is not Communism. Rather, it is common sense. Corporate CEOs, the top-level executives, would still be able to make as many million as they desired. The difference is that they would now have to carry everyone else along. If the enforced compensation ratio was 10:1, for example, if the CEO made $300,000 and the lowest-paid employee $30,000, when the CEO wanted to raise his or her compensation level to $600,000, that person would be required to generate enough new profits to raise the compensation level of the lowest-paid employee to $60,000 at the same time. If unions took the lead in forcing this change, it would be difficult imagining the rest of the workforce not joining in.

Technology: Friend or Foe?

In the same "Opinion Pages" editorial, Krugman talked about the effect of computer technology on the job market. Until the 1700s, technology changed very little. The only way to increase productivity was to put in longer hours. With the rediscovery of "scientific method" and the development of the steam engine, however, this situation changed. Machines were invented that allowed continual growth in production levels. Eventually, more sophisticated machines also began replacing workers. While this phenomenon was seen by many as a threat and jobs as we knew them did disappear, each new technology in terms of the big picture ended up creating more jobs than it replaced.

That is, until the era of the computer. Yes, computers do create new jobs. But computers can also create new computers that can do most of these new jobs more efficiently than humans, cutting costs when in a competitive market cost is considered the most critical factor. Computers are playing an increasingly important role in our economy. In the early days of the United States, a majority of its citizens spent most of their time raising food. Now, less than 10 percent are farmers. Machines now plant, fertilize, and harvest crops. Cows are fed and milked automatically. Chicken eggs are delivered via conveyor belt.

During the Industrial Revolution most laborers held jobs in primary industry—weaving cloth, mining coal, forging steel, manufacturing cars. Now, most of those jobs have been automated, and less than 20 percent of our workforce still earns its pay in this sector. Next came the service industries that currently house a majority of employees. But computers are taking over a growing number of these jobs as well. One alternative is to limit their use. But then, the United States is competing against nations that are already ahead of us in terms of utilizing computers effectively.

There is no doubt that computers are here to stay. We understand now that in order to remain competitive the

United States must continue seeking new ways to use them to cut costs and to increase productivity. The question this need brings up is, What to do with people currently in the workforce and those preparing to join the workforce if the number of jobs available continues to shrink? The question now is how to reorient our economic system, how to reorganize the distribution of wealth so that all people will have continued access to the resources required to develop their potential and to contribute. The question now is how to discover new roles for those who have lost their jobs to technology.

Economists and the government will have to take the lead in meeting the global challenge presented by technology. However, the union movement can play an important part in this effort by educating the public as to what lies down the road and by putting pressure on politicians to start paying attention. Unions could also facilitate the development of training programs for those whose jobs are lost.

Back into the Lead

In summation, three global issues around which to rally the entire workforce have been presented. If unions remain locked into local issues, they will continue to lose their power and their attractiveness. It is time for them to regain the perspective that first made them so important to the development of our society. It is time for them, once again, to begin focusing on challenges important to everybody, challenges such as the need for universal healthcare, the need to get executive salaries under control, and the need to deal with the loss of jobs to technology. Unions are still sorely needed and have a much larger role to play in modern society, if they are willing to take it on.

Chapter 15

Reinterpreting the Concept of Laissez-Faire Economics

In this chapter I shall offer an interpretation of laissez-faire economics that contradicts the one dominant in the US business world today. *I shall explain why many of the serious systemic problems that corporations are currently experiencing result not so much from the laissez-faire approach but from its misinterpretation, from its confusion with egoism, and finally from our failure to update the concept as the workplace culture has evolved.*

The first thing necessary to our argument is a definition of the concept we are discussing. *Laissez-faire economics* has been practiced in varying degrees from the beginning of economic times. It was Adam Smith, however, who formally introduced it to modern, Western society. He described the concept in his 1776 book entitled *Inquiry into the Nature and Causes of the Wealth of Nations,* showing its usefulness and bringing it into the spotlight. Smith said that in terms of economic development the greatest good would come to the greatest number of citizens if government kept its hands off, if business people were allowed to pursue their own self-interests without interference. Smith said that the "natural" law of supply and demand would regulate the marketplace, keeping prices in check.

When asked how the ambitious would be stopped from "messing" with this law of supply and demand, from developing monopolies, from using unethical means to get rid of competition, from lying to the public concerning product quality and their company's financial situation in order to improve individual profits, Smith said that man's "inner good" would provide the necessary constraint.

Adam Smith was not a psychologist; he was an economist. His understanding of the motivators of men was obviously limited. We have learned the hard way that laissez-faire economics, at least in its popular form, does not produce the desired results—the greatest good for the greatest number. What it produces, instead, is an economic plutocracy, a small segment of the population gaining control of the economy and manipulating it to benefit themselves at the expense of the greatest number.

With the Help of Adam Smith the British Get the Ball Rolling

British economic philosophy during the early Industrial Revolution, which began in the late 1700s, was basically laissez-faire. The royal family had been stripped of its power. The Church no longer played a role in governance. Parliament set both social and economic policy, and that body was quickly dominated by industrialists driven by the concept of the economic man, by the belief that the most important objective in life was to make as much money as possible as quickly as possible, no matter what the consequences of your actions to others and to society as a whole.

Without regulation and taxes, great fortunes were, indeed, rapidly amassed. But the degree of deprivation and suffering endured by the laboring classes during this period is unmatched in modern industrial history. Unemployment, workplace accidents, malnutrition and sickness due to low wages and terrible living conditions, laborers beaten if they tired—all these things were commonplace. The "greatest number" was obviously not benefiting from the wealth being generated by the laissez-faire approach, and after approximately 50 years, the British government was forced to step in and start regulating.

The same thing happened in the United States, a nation born into the laissez-faire economic tradition (1776 was a big year for us too). The Civil War, which began in 1860, gave a large boost to the industrialization of the North. Very quickly a small group of the most intelligent, the most ambitious, the most ruthless took control of not only the economy but also of the government. This group, eventually labeled the "robber barons," did indeed develop the country's economic infrastructure. But it did so, once again, at unacceptable expense to the "greatest number." The country suffered a depression or a severe recession approximately every 10 years. Unemployment reached 30 percent. Because the line of applicants at the door was so long (The robber barons supported "Give me your tired, your poor," but for a reason quite different from the one intended by the French when they presented us with the Statue of Liberty) that employers could get away with unreasonably low wages and with unsafe working conditions.

Once again, after approximately 50 years, the US government was forced to step in and to begin regulating. Following Britain's lead it also became socialistic (government controlling or strongly regulating services critical to societal development such as education and transportation, collecting a portion of the wealth generated by industry through taxes and using this portion to support such services) so that the main question now became one of balance. Rather than whether or not an economy should become socialistic, the question to be addressed at this point was exactly *how* socialistic England should become, *how* socialistic the United States and other societies originally practicing laissez-faire economics should become. And equally as important, how socialistic *could* they become without killing incentive?

Putting the Emphasis in the Wrong Place

Does this mean that the laissez-faire philosophy of economic development is fatally flawed? No, it does not. Rather, it means that our *interpretation* of the laissez-faire philosophy is flawed. If we acted the way Adam Smith sought to encourage us to act, laissez-faire would work just fine. His objective was to get rid of the government regulation that stifled efforts to increase profits so that more wealth could be generated and society *as a whole* could benefit, not just the financial elite. He made this very clear in his writings. The problem is that today when we talk about "pursuing our own self-interest," too many of us automatically add, "at the expense of others when necessary," harking all the way back to the days of the Machiavellian humanists mentioned in Chapter 3 and back to the economic man philosophy. But is this necessary? When we focus on our own self-interest, when we try to improve our own situation, does it necessarily have to be at the expense of others?

I think not.

Such a mind-set has more to do with egoism and the scarcity mentality than with laissez-faire economics. *Egoism,* discussed in Chapter 10, is a school of thought that says we should be totally self-centered. In an egotistical world there is no cooperation. One cannot cooperate if one is totally self-centered because cooperation requires compromise and giving, while egoism involves just taking. The only modes of interaction possible when egoism reigns are conflict (no rules) and competition (rules and a referee). If somebody has something you want, you just take it, or you find some way to relieve that person of it according to the rules. If potential investors have the money needed to make the value of your stock options rise, you do whatever is necessary to get them to invest. You cook the books, or you tell them only the part of what is going on that reinforces your sales effort.

Another factor that feeds perfectly into egoism is the *scarcity mentality*. The scarcity mentality, which has played a major role in economic development since the Renaissance, is based on the realization that there is not enough of a needed or desired resource (money) to meet the needs and desires of everyone. As a result, people strive to earn more than they normally require because others will try continually to take away what they have accumulated. People never stop adding to their pile. Their share is never large enough for them to be truly secure. They spend their lives behaving in a paranoid manner, hoarding and worrying, pouring more and more into their coffers, just in case. That is the scarcity mentality.

At the same time, however, we must not forget that some egoism is a necessary thing. Pursuing one's own self-interest is the best incentive of all. This is how people are encouraged to extend themselves. This is how the desire to make improvements is fostered. But what about "the greatest good for the greatest number" part, how does *it* fit? This part of Smith's pronouncement obviously smacks of utilitarianism, which, in the realm of ethical theory, lies at the opposite end of the spectrum from egoism. Those with a utilitarian perspective say that the best decision, the best approach, is that which best satisfies the interests of the majority.

Adam Smith in his writings did something that has confused readers. He combined polar opposites from the world of ethics in his definition of laissez-faire economics. "The greatest good for the greatest number" obviously smacks of utilitarianism, while "will come from each individual pursuing his or her own self-interest" is about as egotistical as it gets. As a result of this confusion, is the approach too flawed to be of use?

Should we forget laissez-faire economics? Is it like an outdated piece of technology that should be shut away in a museum and displayed only as a period piece?

Laissez Faire Adapted to the Modern-Day Workplace

Actually, to me, what Smith has said, in a modern-day context, makes sense. It makes more sense now than it might have in Smith's time. It makes very good sense. The key is the concept of *self-interest*. During Smith's time self-interest had mainly to do with pay. According to the work ethic developed during the Protestant Reformation, as discussed in Chapter 11, people sacrificed their time during working hours, frequently doing repetitious, deadening jobs to earn the money that allowed them to gain physical security and do what they wanted during their nonworking hours. Work included a sacrifice of one's time. The desired reward for that sacrifice was the paycheck.

Today, according to the literature, we still want to earn money for our efforts, but we also want to be respected, to be given a say in decisions that affect us, to be allowed to continue learning while we work. The definition of self-interest, therefore, has expanded as workplace and management systems have evolved.

But what kind of atmosphere allows these things— adequate compensation, respect, empowerment, and continual learning? The answer, of course, is the increasingly popular team approach to work-related decision making and problem solving. Currently, teams of workers generate most of the decisions and most of the wealth produced by organizations. Team efforts are based on mutual respect. The team approach, if mounted correctly, is the best vehicle for empowerment of an organization's members. Teams, more than anything else, are learning vehicles for those involved.

Egoism, of course, does not do well in the team environment. The nature of a team effort makes cooperation and compromise necessary. Team members do not appreciate and do not put up very long with hot dogs, with those whose objective is to use team expertise solely for their own individual gain, to beat the other team members.

So now we have a situation where our self-interest is best pursued by working cooperatively with others. It is extremely obvious to anyone studying modern-day organizations that the ones currently producing the most profit are those where employees work together and support each other, where employees *want* and are encouraged by the reward system to work together and to support each other.

In saying this we also realize that focusing on self-interest no longer necessarily makes us egotistical. Self-interest in the progressive workplace is now most effectively pursued when a more utilitarian attitude is adopted. But more importantly, our changed definition of self-interest and of the most effective way to pursue it feeds right into Smith's "the greatest good for the greatest number." Obviously, if you and I are working as a team, the fulfillment of my self-interest is tied to the fulfillment of your self-interest. If I am going to fulfill mine, I am going to have to help you fulfill yours as well. It has also been recognized that, at least for most of us, if we work together, if we share our expertise, we are going to achieve our objectives faster.

A New Start?

According to our reinterpretation of Smith's original definition of laissez-faire economics, therefore, "the greatest good for the greatest number" does indeed come from encouraging employees to pursue their own self-interest. The best way to pursue my own self-interest in the modern workplace is to integrate my efforts with those of my other team members and for my team to integrate its efforts effectively with those of the other teams in the organization.

If this attitude, perchance, spreads throughout the business world, they will further benefit themselves. If corporations and other organizations as well start to cooperate rather than constantly battle (as is beginning to happen), their objective being to benefit society and in doing so would benefit themselves, the need for government regulation will diminish; additionally, the laissez-faire approach to economics will most likely experience a revival because the general public will embrace the new version.

The possibility of this happening is not as outlandish as it might sound to some, with corporations that have historically been at each other's throats beginning to cooperate, to share expertise and resources. W. Edwards Deming predicted some 30 years ago that such a shift would eventually come to pass, that it *must* come to pass. And what he said makes sense, not only because of the synergies that will be generated but also as a way of better utilizing resources. And, no, we are not talking about communism. The government is not in control, not making the decisions as to which company can produce what, as to how much they can produce, and what price they can charge. The companies themselves will still be making the critical decisions, but in such a way that each will benefit, probably more so than if they were still fighting it out.

In summation, then, what our businesses and employees need in order to excel in modern times is to, indeed, adopt the laissez-faire approach—reinterpreted according to our new understanding of the concept of self-interest. The laissez-faire economic system of the future will be based mainly on cooperation rather than on conflict or competition.

Bibliography

Ackoff, R. (1971) Toward a System of Systems Concepts, *Management Sciences*, Vol. 3, No. 11, pp. 661–671.

Ackoff, R. (1999) *Re-Creating the Corporation: A Design of Organizations for the 21st Century*. Oxford, UK: Oxford University Press.

Ackoff, R. (1994) *The Democratic Corporation*. New York: Oxford University Press.

Ackoff, R. & Emery, F. (1972) *On Purposeful Systems*. New York: Aldine-Atherton.

Aguayo, R. (1990) *Dr. Deming: The American Who Taught the Japanese about Quality*. New York: Carol Publishing Group.

Capuano, T. and Roth, W. (Spring 2001) "Systemic versus Non-Systemic Approaches to Quality Improvement," *Journal of Organizational Excellence*, Vol. 20, No. 2, pp. 57–64.

Churchman, W. (1968) *The Systems Approach*. New York: Delacorte Press.

Deming, W. E. (1986) *Out of Crisis*. Boston, MA: MIT Press.

Drucker, P. (1993) *The Concept of the Corporation*. Piscataway, NJ: Transaction Publishers.

Ford, H. (1922) *My Life and Work*. Salem, NH: Ayer Company Publishers.

Gharajedaghi, J. (1984) "On the Nature of Development," *Human Systems Management,* Vol. 4, No. 4.

Gharajedaghi, J. (August 1984) "Organizational Implications of Systems Thinking: Multidimensional Modular Design," *European Journal of Operations Research*, Vol. 18, No. 2.

Goudreau, J. (February 25, 2013) "Back to the Stone Age?" www.forbes.com

Hammer, Michael (1995) *The Reengineering Revolution: A Handbook*. New York: HarperCollins Publishers.

Ivry, R. B. and Robertson, L. C. (1998) *The Two Sides of Perception*. Cambridge, MA: MIT Press.

Kakar, S. (1970) *Frederick Taylor: A Study in Personality and Innovation*. Cambridge MA: MIT Press.

Kanigel, R. (2005) *The One Best Way: Frederick Winslow Taylor and the Enigma of Efficiency*. Boston: MIT Press.

Klopp, S., and Roth, W. (July 1997) "A Systems Approach to Training," *The Journal for Quality and Participation*, Vol. 20, No. 3.

Kruse, K. (December 2012) "Top Ten Benefits of Working from Home (Survey Results)," *Forbes*, Vol. 99, No. 4.

Laslow, E. (1978) *The Relevance of General Systems Theory*. New York: George Baziller Press.

Maslow, A. (1970). *Motivation and Personality*. New York: Harper & Row.

Maslow, A. (1998) *Maslow on Management*. New York: John Wiley and Sons.

Midgley, G. (2000) *Systemic Intervention: Philosophy, Methodology, and Practice*. London: Kluwer Academic/Plenum Publishers.

Pande, P., Neuman, R., and Cavanagh, R. (2000) *The 6-Sigma Way: How GE, Motorola and Other Top Companies Are Honing Their Performance*. New York: McGraw-Hill Press.

Potts, M., and Roth, W. (February 2001) "Doing It Wrong: A Case Study," *Quality Progress*, Vol. 34, No. 2.

Pydzek, T. (2003) *The Six Sigma Handbook: The Complete Guide for Greenbelts, Blackbelts, and Managers at All Levels*. New York: McGraw Hill Press.

Robbins, S. P., & Judge, T. A. (2012) *Essentials of Organization Behavior*. Upper Saddle River, NJ: Pearson Prentice Hall.

Rogers, D. (November 11, 2005) "Answers to Big Three's 'Black October' Is People, Says Pat Carrigan," www.mybaycity.com, Business Article 934.

Roth, W. (September 1990) "A New Role for Unions," *The Journal for Quality and Participation*, Vol. 13, No. 5.

Roth, W. (Summer 2002) "Business Ethics: Grounded in Systems Thinking," *Journal of Organizational Excellence*, Vol. 21, No. 3.

Roth, W. (2010) *Comprehensive Healthcare for the U.S.: An Idealized Model*. Boca Raton, FL: CRC Press.

Roth, W. (September 2000) "Dealing with the Corporate Hotdogs," *The Journal for Quality and Participation*, Vol. 23, No. 4.

Roth, W. (August 1990) "Dos and Don'ts of Quality Improvement," *Quality Progress*, Vol. 23, No. 8.

Roth, W. (March 1988) "Do Safety Programs Really Work?" *Pulp and Paper International*, Vol. 30, No. 3.

Roth, W. (Summer 2009) "Downsizing: The Cure That Can Kill," *Global Business and Organizational Excellence*, Vol. 28, No. 6.

Roth, W. (July 1999) "Enriching the NLRB's Perspective," *Forward Thinking*, Vol. 2, No. 6.

Roth, W. (2005) *Ethics in the Workplace: A Systems Perspective.* Upper Saddle River, NJ: Pearson Prentice Hall.

Roth, W. (Spring 2000) "Getting Beyond the Myth of the Bell Shaped Density Curve," *National Productivity Review,* Vol. 19, No. 2.

Roth, W. (May 1989) "Get Training out of the Classroom," *Quality Progress*, Vol. 22, No. 5.

Roth, W. (1997) "Going All the Way with Empowerment," *TQM Magazine,* Vol. 9, No. 1.

Roth, W. (August 1991) "How to Play the Teambuilding Game," *Pulp and Paper International*, Vol. 33, No. 8.

Roth, W. (October 1991) "IP Takes the Five Phase Approach," *Pulp and Paper International*, Vol. 33, No. 10.

Roth, W. (September 1993) "Is It Quality Improves Ethics or Ethics Improves Quality?" *The Journal for Quality and Participation*, Vol. 16, No. 5.

Roth, W. (Spring 2009) "Is Management by Objective Obsolete?" *Global Business and Organizational Excellence*, Vol. 28, No. 4.

Roth, W. (January 1998) "Middle Management: The Missing Link," *TQM Magazine*, Vol. 10, No. 1.

Roth, W. (1998). *Quality Improvement: A Systems Perspective.* Boca Raton, FL: St. Lucie Press.

Roth, W. (January 1991) "Quality: Rebirth of the Systems Approach," *Quality Digest*, Vol. 11, No. 1.

Roth, W. (2013) "Six-Sigma: Just More of the Same?" *Performance Improvement Journal*, Vol. 52, No. 2.

Roth, W. (October 1994) "The End of Performance Appraisals?" *Quality Digest*, Vol. 14, No. 9.

Roth, W. (1999) *The Roots and Future of Management Theory: A Systems Perspective.* Boca Raton, FL: St. Lucie Press.

Roth, W. (Nov/Dec 1993) "The Slippery Slope," *TQM Magazine*, Vol. 5, No. 6.

Roth, W. (Spring 2002) "Three Reasons Why Your Teambuilding Efforts Aren't Producing," *The Journal for Quality and Participation*, Vol. 25, No. 1.

Roth, W. (October 17, 2004) "Time for Universal Health Care Services," *The Morning Call,* Opinion Section.

Roth, W. (December 1989) "Try Some Quality Improvement Process Glue," *The Journal for Quality and Participation*, Vol. 12, No. 4.

Roth, W. (October 2013) "Who Makes the Most Productive Executive?" *Global Business and Organizational Excellence*, Vol. 52, No. 9.

Roth, W. (February 2014). "From Leadership to Playing Catch-up," *Business Management Dynamics*, Vol. 3, No. 8, pp. 13–17.

Roth, W. (June 1991) "Why Aren't Leaders Leading?" *The Journal for Quality and Participation*, Vol. 14, No. 3.

Roth, W. (Autumn 1998) "Work Ethics," *National Productivity Review*, Vol. 17. No. 4.

Roth, W. (1989) *Work and Rewards: Redefining Our Work-Life Reality*. New York: Praeger.

Schon, D. (1971) *Beyond the Stable State*. London: TempleSmith.

Sellers, P. (October 29, 2012) "Marissa Mayer: Ready to Rumble," *Fortune Magazine*, Vol. 166, No. 7.

Special report (May 12, 1990) "Manager Out at GM Plant," *New York Times*.

Stayer, R. (November/December 1990) "How I Learned to Let My Workers Lead," *Harvard Business Review*, Vol. 68, No. 6.

Stokes, P. (2010) *Philosophy: The Great Thinkers*. London: Arcturus Publishing Ltd.

Tarrant, J. (1976) *Drucker: The Man Who Invented Corporate Society*. Boston: Cahners Books.

Trist, E. (1980) The Evolution of Socio-Technical Systems, *Issues in the Quality of Working Life, No 2,* Ontario, Canada: Ontario Ministry of Labor.

Trist, E., Higgins, G. W., Murray, H., and Pollock, A. B. (1963) *Organizational Choice*. London: Tavistock Publications.

Von Bertalanffy, L. (1962) "General Systems Theory: A Critical Review," *General Systems,* Vol. VII.

Walton, M. (1990) *Deming: Management at Work*. New York: Perigree Books.

Index